The Good, the Bad and the Irritating

and the Irritating

A practical approach for parents of children who are
attention seeking.

by Dr Nigel Mellor
Illustrations by Thir

ISBN 1 873942 43 5

Published by Lucky Duck Publishing Ltd.
3, Thorndale Mews, Clifton, Bristol BS8 2HX

www.luckyduck.co.uk

Designed by Helen Weller
Printed by The Book Factory, Mildmay Avenue, London N1 4RS

Reprinted December 2001, January 2002, March 2002, January 2003

For Eric

Acknowledgements

My heartfelt appreciation is offered to all those parents described in these pages who worked so hard for their children.

Warm thanks is extended to innumerable colleagues and friends who helped check the manuscript, and who, over many years, gave such excellent advice. Particular credit must go to the editors at Lucky Duck and our creative cartoonist.

Extra special gratitude is due to my late colleague Eric Harvey who originally developed this approach to working with families. Without the example of his extraordinary skills, this book would never have been conceived. I owe him a great deal.

Contents

Notes

- The pronoun "we" is used freely throughout the book, hopefully not in any patronising way but to capture all of our experiences as parents, sharing in the same difficulties from time to time.

- Children are referred to as he or she in turn, to avoid the impression that only boys have problems.

- Children are also referred to, at times, as kids. This is not meant to be a demeaning term. We can still respect them as individuals with their own rights and dignity. I trust the descriptions and tales are seen in the same light. I hope that the overall picture presented of the children is positive, although at times it may be embedded in lots of negative emotions. At the end of the day, these are very rewarding children. Coming to see all their positive qualities may, however, involve going through something of a pain barrier.

- An extremely wide range of behaviour difficulties is discussed in this book. I trust the common thread linking them all will become apparent. In addition, connections are made to what appear at first sight to be learning difficulties - see for instance Ann Miller and Philip Gardner's reading problems in the case studies in the appendix.

- Finally, the parents described here were not "bad" parents. Quite the reverse. These were good parents, desperate to do the right thing. But their very concern made them even more vulnerable to the tactics of the attention seeking children. If they had not cared about the children they would not have had these troubles. In their misunderstanding of a very perplexing situation they made mistakes. It can be easy to see the problem from the outside. When you're in the middle of things it's not so easy.

The aim of the book is not to heap guilt on parents for turning out children who are less than perfect. Perfection is not the goal. The aim is to help tackle a very common, but nevertheless extremely difficult and often misunderstood problem: attention seeking. These children present some of the most frustrating difficulties families will ever encounter. Their intensely irritating behaviours, paradoxically, often become worse the harder parents try to deal with them. Ironically, such predicaments are encountered by the most dedicated adults. As **Mr Oswald** complained about his 6 year old son **Jordan**, who we'll meet again later: "I've tried coaxing, punishing, ignoring. It doesn't make a damn bit of difference."

The catch with attention seeking children is that your normal approaches don't seem to work.

Introduction

There can be a thousand and one reasons for a child's behaviour to give us concern. It is obviously vitally important to rule out medical conditions. For instance, a child with an undiagnosed hearing loss may appear to be deliberately naughty.

Some of these difficulties may be very short lived, others may drag on for months before righting themselves. All the difficulties we could meet from time to time do not need equally massive amounts of help to clear them up.

A child may be upset because of illness; because of worrying about bullying; because of some medication they are taking; because school work is too hard; because we are expecting too much; because a teacher is unsympathetic; because Uncle Joe just died; because parents are divorcing; because he is frustrated about his physical disability; because she is going through a perfectly normal phase of adolescent rebellion and so on. Each of these needs rather different handling and there is no magic wand to clear away all the troubles of childhood.

Children's behaviour can cause concern in the best of environments, but problems can often be overcome with a whole range of simple, everyday approaches which we use almost automatically : talk to her about her worries; distract her when the oldest one goes out; avoid the toy counter in John Lewis; help her talk through her frustrations; involve him in digging the garden with you if he's jealous of the baby and so on.

It may need a chat to her teacher or a change of class or separating him from someone who triggers him off. We don't always need a sledgehammer to crack a nut.

Unfortunately, sometimes matters seem to spiral out of control. Whatever we do, the problem does not improve, in fact sometimes the harder we try the worse it seems to be. We feel our relationship with the child rapidly deteriorating as his behaviour becomes more outrageous and annoying. Our best efforts may achieve nothing, but leave us frustrated and exhausted.

In that case we may be meeting what is in fact a very common problem. It is, however, one which is very difficult to tackle unless we can see the pattern behind what may appear to be very puzzling and unconnected events.

The method described in the following pages obviously may not be right for any particular child. It is always important, where possible, to seek expert advice.

Again, the approach may be exactly right but because of the situation we find ourselves in we just cannot apply it, like the woman struggling alone at home with a large family on a low income or the parent filled with guilt and worries about having a disabled child or the parents driven to breaking point and at their wits' end.

Do not feel any single approach is either totally right or totally wrong for any child or that all problems require the same solution. Use these ideas only if it seems appropriate and things are getting out of hand.

N.B. If you suspect a more serious matter such as major learning difficulties, depression, eating disorders or other marked psychiatric conditions, severe bullying or abuse, always seek professional help.

Chapter 1

Explanations for misbehaviour

Why do children behave the way they do? In particular, why do they misbehave? Let's rule out the obvious things first, such as feeling off colour or being understandably upset by the death of someone very close. Let us just consider the child whose behaviour has been very worrying and unacceptable over a long period of time despite our best efforts to change it.

First of all we must be aware of the half-conscious, half-formed ideas we carry around in our heads to explain behaviour problems. These get in the way every time we start to try to deal with misbehaviour even though we may not be fully aware of them.

There are lots of these half thought-out explanations. It is important to examine them closely and realise they may be forming a barrier to taking effective action.

Here are just a few examples:

The primitive explanation for misbehaviour

"It's in the blood" or "His Uncle Jim was the same - it comes through on

Primitive Explanation

Just like her dad

9

your mother's side." In other words, there isn't much anyone can do. They were born that way so you might as well lock them up and throw away the key.

The psychiatric explanation for misbehaviour

A vague idea about what Freud said. Something to do with the child not having passed through various stages of development such as the anal stage or not having resolved his Oedipus complex. Or we might say his mean, cold nature is due to severe potty training at age two or... .... (add your own comments, preferably in a German accent, it sounds more convincing).

The psychological explanation for misbehaviour

It is difficult to put your finger on exactly what this is. It seems tied up with ideas about flows of information and funny little concepts like "short term memory" all mixed up with the magic ingredient I.Q. We then make allowances for the child behaving in

Psychiatric Explanation
"There, there son"
▶ *Mother dominated.*
Oral fixation. Potty hang-ups.

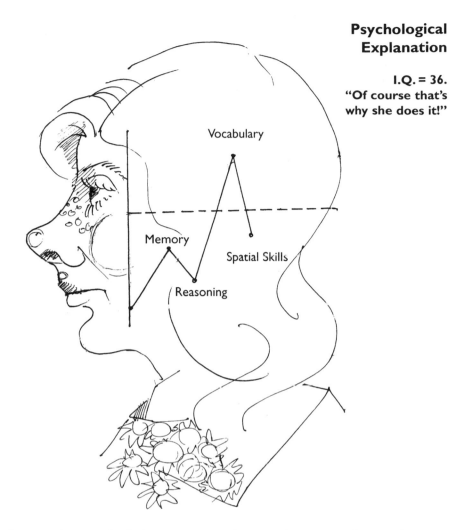

**Psychological
Explanation**

**I.Q. = 36.
"Of course that's
why she does it!"**

peculiar ways because she isn't very bright. A variation on this theme is to make excuses for her misbehaviour because she is extremely intelligent and "highly strung." However, both are inappropriate.

The disabilities explanation for misbehaviour

This isn't a real theory at all. It is just a collection of ideas that add up to saying that certain disabilities by themselves explain away behaviour difficulties. You might, for instance, hear people comment incorrectly, "What do you expect from a girl with Down's Syndrome?"

We may be carrying round a collection of confused ideas. Nicholas Noble, age 14, for instance was very difficult at home and school. When we dig around, mum's comments reveal she is actually toying with several possible explanations all at the same time:

"He can be good but he just has "radgie" [bad-tempered] days. I wonder if it's the food. With his weight and glasses, they're skitting

Disabilities
Explanation

**"Don't worry – it's just
de Brugel-Smitzer
Konigberg syndrome"**

him all the time. Last year his grandma died. A baby died when he was two; was he too young for that to have any influence? He just likes being the centre of attention. Can't we hypnotise him?"

There are lots more of these "explanations." Unfortunately they don't help us because they don't tell us what we can do to help the child. After all, if it's "in the blood" or "in the genes" then there's not much anyone can do about it.

So, what is going on?

Read on

Chapter 2

A useful explanation for misbehaviour

Did you ever play a game when you were kids where you knock on some poor soul's door then run away chuckling? The grown up comes out screaming and shouting. He thinks that will put you off. At least that's how it appears through the adult's eyes.

Let's view things through the children's eyes. They want the adult to come out. The more he shouts and screams, the more fun it is. As soon as he goes back in, still hopping mad, the kids come back and knock again. They've got the adult on a string.

"I'll kill you, you little b****!"**

So when we see things through the child's eyes the behaviour starts to make sense.

But what's all this got to do with misbehaviour?

It seems that some children at some point in their lives develop a great need for attention. If you like, a kind of hunger. They just have to make adults take notice of them, talk to them, stare at them, even moan at them, shout, reason or argue. In other words, spend time with them and no one else. It's all attention through the child's eyes. As we will see, they use misbehaviour to achieve a response, to "knock on your door."

O.K. I can go along with that. But why does it start?

We can't turn the clock back and there is little point dwelling on ancient history. That usually just piles up guilt. However, there are some possible "trigger points" in the past which could have started off the child's great hunger for attention. Just for interest's sake, I've listed a few below:

Trigger points

For some children, everything is O.K. till a new baby comes along. Suddenly they find that are no longer the centre of attention, the little stranger is. Then they find that "acting up" retrieves the attention they were missing out on.

Or he's O.K. until he's five and it's time to start school. He's tearful. We are worried and give him more attention when he cries and complains. That's quite natural. There's nothing wrong in that for most kids, but some just happen to go on and become locked into the cycle of crying, complaining etc. to obtain attention.

Or she goes into hospital and when she comes out she's clingy and upset. We are very worried and feed in extra attention because of our (quite natural) anxieties. But for some kids "the penny drops" and the habit of seeking attention in inappropriate ways starts off the vicious circle.

Or we go through a difficult patch in our marriage (haven't we all!). The children react badly. We respond and everything spirals out of control as we over-react or, through feeling guilty, make more and more allowances for unreasonable behaviour.

Or the child goes through a phase of not eating and we become very worried and make a big scene every mealtime.

Or the child has been adopted or fostered so we try to make up for the past and make too many allowances.

As one mum commented about her 14 year old, "She's had more than the other two children put together." Mum went on to say, "She's also been ruined by the others...we haven't really done her any favours. I've never really had any trouble with the other two... am I making a mistake?" Dad had been

14

saying, "You spoil her" but mum explained, "It's my way of compensating." One of the older children had been very ill and had absorbed a great deal of the family's energies.

There can be thousands of reasons: the onset of puberty; a change of schools; worrying about cot deaths so we check the baby every five minutes and soon he can't sleep without dad there; picking the baby up every time she cries so that soon we can't put her down and so on.

But what I can't figure out is why this one went wrong. We treated them all the same.

Parents often say "We brought them all up the same, why is this one different?" But children aren't cans of peas, churned out by the million, all identical. They are individuals. While wanting to be seen to be even-handed, and not showing favouritism, parents do tailor their approaches to their children. One child might lack confidence, one might be more lively, one might have more appetite. We subtly adjust our style to suit.

Anyway, in reality, children don't receive the same handling. Each child's experience of the family is unique: one child has an older brother, but the older one has a younger brother. Children come into the family at different times of stress, and experience different events. One child may remind us of someone we don't like. With later born children we may be more

experienced, but more tired. From the first few days of life, research shows that we do not react to girls and boys quite the same way. Even twins can differ in subtle but crucial ways in their reactions. And all these tiny variations can make a large impact on our parenting, and the child's responses.

It is sometimes hard to understand how such small differences can have such profound effects. The connection may be like the beating of the butterfly's wing in Tokyo which leads to the hurricane in New York. Starting with some remote, perhaps quite insignificant event, the child very gradually becomes more and more irritating to seek attention. The parents gradually become more and more annoyed in response. These interactions then feed on each other and spiral out of control. No one is to blame. No one could predict the sequence of events. No one wanted it to happen.

Now, none of the triggers mentioned might apply to the particular child we are concerned about. Some of these triggers may happen to any child and yet the great need for attention may not arise. As we said above, we cannot turn the clock back and say exactly what caused the problem at what time. All we can do is deal with the situation in the here and now. The important point is that at some time in the child's life, she becomes locked into a vicious circle. She needs attention. Misbehaviour brings attention, so she carries on in that way. But the solution does not lie in raking over the past.

▶ *See for example case studies of David Fox p.71 (going into care and into hospital gave plenty of opportunity to trigger off his need for attention) or Debbie Tait p.63 and Colin*

Hurd p.75 (going into hospital) or George Parker p.60 (mum's guilt about George and the birth of a new baby probably set the ball rolling). The interviews however did not dwell on whether or not these were "triggers", it makes little difference in any case years later. The point is, to consider what we can do about it today.

Does this mean it's all our fault – we're just bad parents?

No. We all have different ideas on how to bring up children and, on the whole, do a pretty good job. As was noted earlier, "perfection" is not the goal. However, the average child would drive a saint to distraction and it's not that we're bad parents if we slip up from time to time. After all, how much training were we given to be parents? None! Even the simplest job in town has some training provided. Being a parent, the most important job in the world, has least. The baby's dumped in your lap and it's "get on with it." It's not surprising we make mistakes with that most puzzling problem of all: attention seeking.

But I still don't see how this explains my Darren's awful behaviour!

Read on...

```
VACANCY

JOB TITLE: Parent

JOB DESCRIPTION: On call permanently, to
meet the slightest whims of egocentric,
irrational small persons.

CONDITIONS:    No guaranteed rest breaks. No
               back-up. No thanks. Buy your
               own equipment.

HOURS:         24 hours per day.

HOLIDAYS:      Nil.

TRAINING:      Nil.

PAY:           Nil.

LENGTH OF CONTRACT:   21 years.
```

Chapter 3

We all need attention

"Reginald, dear, look who's
coming to stay!"

We all need attention and we don't want to share it with an interloper. Any attention coming from our partners we want for ourselves. We don't want half.

Kids are just the same. They find it very hard to share adult's attention. Unfortunately, some kids don't just want attention, they're desperate for it. And they find out very early on in life that the easiest way to grab attention is to be a nuisance.

Go on - be honest

We know, if we're honest with ourselves, that if our child is sitting playing nicely in the other room we'll tend to say "Thank heaven he's quiet" and carry on with the dishes in peace.

For most kids, most of the time, there's no harm in that. If, however, that child, after some trigger or other, has become hungry for attention, he'll find out very early on that sitting quietly isn't the way to get it.

So what can he do? Rip the book up rather than read it. Knock the TV over. Argue with his brothers and sisters. Annoy the cat. Bang on the windows. Scream as if he's dying. These bring parents in pretty quickly.

Take this list of behaviours for instance. What do they all have in common?

Swears. Argues back at you. Tantrums. Goes on and on about sweets. Claims you're always picking on him. Refuses to tell you what he's upset about. Fidgets. Is noisy and active all the time. Cheeky. Untidy. Says "I'm bored." Steals. Breaks toys. Picks his nose. Blinks her eyes. Acts the clown. Bites his nails. Twitches his face.

Cracks her fingers. Screams. Won't eat. Scared of the dark. Dawdles when getting ready. Wets the bed. Deliberately does the opposite of what he was asked to. Speaks very loudly. Sulks. Moody. Threatens to run away. Slams the door. Leaves toys all over the place. Drops clothes on the floor. Refuses to get washed. Says he's ill every school day. Loses her timetable every day. "Switches off" when asked about her behaviour. Lights fires. Smirks at you and gives off-hand responses when questioned. Stays out all night. Argues with his sister. Always "on the want." Doesn't work at school. Rejects your help when you offer it. Dives into the sea as soon as she reaches the beach. Runs along the top of the wall. Mumbles. Says she hates school. Runs across the road. Dies his hair purple. Is accident prone. Truants. Wears ear rings. Smashes windows. Belches. Swings on the door. Cries. Always appears very timid. Won't wash. Tells tales. Mixes with the wrong kind of friends. Talks like a baby. Watches cartoons all day. Smears faeces. Wastes money on ice-creams. Spits. Spends all day on computer games. Is very aggressive to small children. Eats soil. Hits her head on the wall. Rocks back and forth...

They are all very different, but they do have one thing in common. They immediately bring a great deal of attention.

For instance, visualise the average child coming in from school. She slams the door. What do mum or dad say?: "Don't do that, how many times have I told you, you'll break the glass."

There's one lump of attention

Then she drops her coat on the floor. "Pick it up, this isn't a pig-sty. It cost me thirty pounds last week and you're treating it like an old rag already. You never take care of your clothes."

There's two lumps of attention

Then she walks along the corridor leaving muddy footprints. "For heaven's sake, clean your shoes. Do I have to tell you every time you come in. I've been working all day trying to clean this place and now see the mess you've made."

There's three lumps of attention and she's hardly through the door yet.

Then it goes on throughout the evening. Arguing with her brother. Turning the TV up too loudly. These bring immediate attention.

What does she say at tea time? "I hate that. I'm not eating that stuff." So how do we react? We try to encourage her to eat, tell her it'll be good for her and so on. In other words we feed in massive amounts of attention.

Then she's up and down and fidgeting in her seat. "For heaven's sake, will you sit still. Have you got ants in your pants?"

So there's seven lumps of attention she's had before six o'clock.

She can go on the whole evening and never repeat herself. Each one of these behaviours seems very different, and in many ways they are. *But they all have one thing in common:* they immediately bring massive amounts of adult attention.

Now I've got the picture. Getting attention is the key to it all.

Yes, that's the main driving force. But there are some others, as the next chapter shows.

Chapter 4

The pay-offs for misbehaving

There are other "rewards" that misbehaviour can bring. **Attention** is the major one and we'll concentrate on this for most of the book. There are two main, extra pay-offs, however, which explain some of the problems we face: she may also be creaming off **entertainment** and a feeling of **power**.

If we think back to our own school days when we had boring maths on a dreary Friday afternoon. It was much more fun to drive the teacher crazy by scraping the chair or making silly noises and have him hopping up and down. With luck we avoided a thick ear while brightening up a dull hour.

It's the same for the child at home. Sometimes we find he's driving us crazy. We're chasing after him. We'll murder him if we catch him, yet he's laughing. It's exciting. It's better than East Enders! The misbehaviour brings the reward of **entertainment**. The child doesn't have to sit and plan this, he just gradually, almost unconsciously, discovers it over a period of time.

But there is another possible pay-off (which may again be totally unplanned on the child's part): the feeling of **power**.

Do you like complaining, shouting at, telling off, "going on" at your child? No, of course not. He makes you do something you don't want to do. For that moment he's in charge.

Remember, we all like the feeling of power. Kids are no different. Even without consciously trying to work out how to do it, children can still enjoy the feeling that they have us on a string.

▶ *All of the case studies show the variety of ways children can obtain attention, see for example Keith Frost p.59 (sucking his thumb, biting his nails and dawdling were very effective). In many instances the children are clearly being "irritating" for attention. Some also discover less obvious ways such as the powerful effect of failing to make progress e.g. George Parker p.60 or simply refusing to talk e.g. Ann Miller p.65.*

Surely you're not saying she likes being told off?

No. But let's look at things through the child's eyes for a moment. Misbehaviour might or might not lead to a punishment. How many of us always carry out our threats?
▸ *See for example Keith Frost p.59 (mum wanted to avoid punishment most of the time) or Debbie Tait p.63 (Mr Tait saw her as "his little baby").*

In the meantime the child soaks up three very powerful rewards: Attention, Entertainment and a feeling of Power.

If he's hungry for attention then to him it starts to make sense to misbehave. It pays off. It brings him exactly what he needs with only a small chance of being punished - apart from being shouted at (which is just another form of attention and to many kids is just like water off a duck's back anyway).What happens if, for instance, he just sits quietly reading a book. What would we say to him? We might say nothing, or we might say one or two words in a very low key, off-hand way ... "There's a good lad."

It's not enough. The child sees a tiny amount of attention coming to him if he behaves well and a much much greater amount if he misbehaves.
▸ *See, for example, how readily Andy West p.69, John Utting p.81 and Colin Hurd p.75 could recall criticism but not praise, and how Colin's parents focused on his irritating behaviour.*

To the child it makes perfect sense to misbehave. It brings exactly what he needs at that point in time. We put a lot of feeling and emotion into telling children off. We rarely put as much effort into praising them. We tend to do that in a very low key manner and run out of things to say pretty quickly. Through the child's eyes, this smidgen of praise is not much in the way of attention.

So, what can we do about it?

There is an approach that works. But it isn't easy. The approach is like a pair of scissors. We need both blades to cut. One blade on its own is not enough. Similarly this method has two "blades" or two parts to it. These must be used together.

People who try this without advice, often miss out one or other part. Then they say "I've tried that and it didn't work." If we persist with both parts, however, the technique is very effective.

The basic idea is to make sure that the child receives very little attention for unacceptable behaviour. That's one blade of the scissors. The other half of the approach, the other blade of the scissors (which is often overlooked) is to make sure that when we do give him attention it is in large amounts and for the behaviour we want.

That sounds easy. It isn't. So be prepared for a few more grey hairs before you're through.

But aren't we just treating the symptoms?

No. What we find is that *the attention seeking is the problem*. It is not the sign of some deeper disturbance that needs three years of counselling or a cocktail of drugs to "cure." There is simply a spiral which, after some trigger or series of events, lost in history, runs out of control. The child produces more and more negative, sometimes quite bizarre, behaviours. The parents respond to these, giving more and more attention.

The feeling of power

As one author describes:

"…the bizarre behaviour was the problem; his "disturbance" was no more nor no less than the bizarre behaviour, and was not some separate underlying entity that we should assume existed as well"
▸ see Morgan 1984 p.3, in further reading section.

We can only guess at the mechanism that initiates this. But how the spiral starts is not important. What is important is that we know that, if parents adopt the kind of programme described in this book, the problem eventually goes away. The child does not become an angel, but matters settle down to just the normal round of childhood difficulties. The intensively destructive, escalating cycle of seeking attention through more and more misbehaviour, is broken.

We need to tackle this "vicious circle" in two parts:

(1) The first part, the first blade of the scissors: What we do about the child's misbehaviour.

(2) The second part, the other blade of the scissors, the part that's often forgotten: What we do about the child's good behaviour.

Let's think about misbehaviour first. Remember, the main idea is to give as little attention as possible to misbehaviour, to ignore it where we can. That doesn't mean, however, that we should ignore everything. There are some things we cannot ignore. For instance, if your child throws a brick through the window, you can't ignore that.

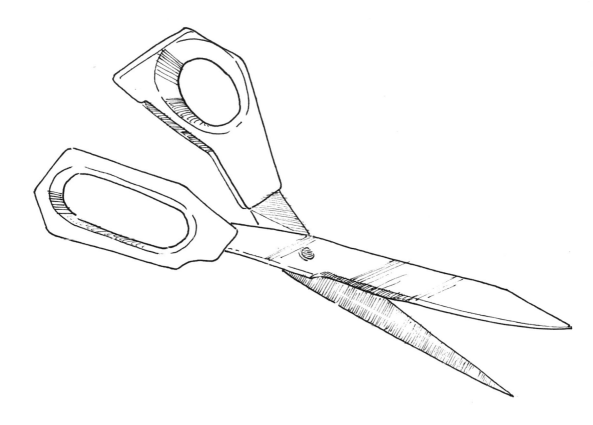

What should we do then, if she misbehaves? First, we make an instant decision whether this is something we could ignore or whether it is something we have to take action over, put in a small punishment for instance.

Now both of these, ignoring and punishing, are difficult to do well. We'll discuss them in much more detail in the next four chapters. However, the second blade of the scissors - what we do about the good behaviour, the use of praise and other rewards - is also surprisingly difficult to do well. We'll examine this in chapters 9 and 10.

At times we all use bits of the approach. The trick is, however, to sharpen up each part and to make the parts work together smoothly. Just like a pair of scissors, one blade on its own is no use at all, no matter how sharp it is.

The following chapters concentrate on just those three basic techniques which sound so simple: ignoring, punishing and praising.

Chapter 5

Ignoring

If we decide to try to ignore some minor piece of irritating behaviour we must first be aware that this is actually one of the hardest parts of the approach. I want to spend a great deal of time examining this aspect. This repeated, microscopic focus on tiny details is essential. The most "obvious" techniques are those we most often miscalculate, simply because they seem so easy. But they aren't.

Most children can read adults like a book. They know our every emotion. They know exactly what gets under our skin and when to have the maximum effect (when it's most inconvenient for us, naturally). It's not that they plan this. They aren't clones of a Child of the Devil. They just learn it, almost by accident, over a period of time.

We are fairly good at reading other people's emotions ourselves. Think of the last time you went to visit some friends. They had just had a row. Even though they're not shouting at each other when you walk in, you can feel the atmosphere. You can cut the air with a knife.

Children are even better at picking up emotions than we are. Over the years they find out which things most annoy adults. We've all got our vulnerable points and they are different for each person. The child stumbles across these. He doesn't decide to annoy us deliberately. He just gradually discovers that certain pieces of irritating behaviour will bring him what he wants: attention.

▶ *See for example how Mrs Fox showed her emotions clearly on her face p.71.*

We usually give the game away in any case. When he scrapes his shoes over and over again, for example, or does something else that particularly irritates us, we end up red in the face shouting "For heaven's sake, will you stop that." But what we have done in effect is to put up a big sign saying: "That's the one to do again if you want attention, it makes me so mad."

We're all human. We are all vulnerable somewhere. Children don't have to be very clever to find these spots. Remember, they have nothing else to think about. We, on the other hand, are constantly thinking about a dozen things at once: The car needs fixing. Little Patrick's shoes are falling apart. The roof's leaking. Sinead wants a new coat. How can we afford to go to Greece this year? Children have none of these worries.

So over the weeks and months and years, children readily discover what drives us insane. They have nothing else to distract them. That's why they seem to "win" so easily: they can concentrate on number one. They aren't selfish, they're just kids. We need to work at ignoring.

Training yourself to ignore

We have to think about *training ourselves to ignore*. That sounds something of a contradiction, but we need to be clear what ignoring means and how to ignore. It's not as easy as it sounds.

- Ignoring means don't look at the child when he performs the irritating behaviour (such as cracking his knuckles or fidgeting or nail biting).

Don't make any comments about it.

- If you really have to make some comment, for instance to stop him fiddling with the television set, keep your voice as calm and level as possible. Say as little as possible. Make sure your body and face are relaxed and not showing any tension so that the message the you have actually been annoyed does not come across. That physical tension shows itself in a kind of "body language" which can give the game away even more strongly than words.

Ignoring is difficult for many reasons

1. You have to keep it up.

Imagine you ignore his nose picking on Monday, Tuesday, Wednesday, Thursday... then on Saturday you crack and start to scream. All your week's work has been in vain. The reason is simple enough once you view it from the outside.

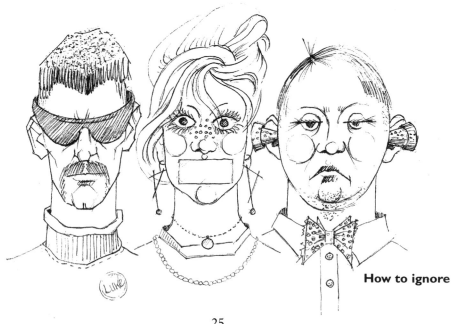

How to ignore

25

The child sees you like a one-armed bandit. You put your money in Monday, Tuesday, Wednesday and nothing comes out. Then Saturday night, you hit the jackpot. So you think to yourself "We're back in business" and keep on playing. The swindle is, the people who make the one-armed bandits are very cute. They programme the machines so that they pay out just often enough to keep you hooked. Gamblers don't get rich generally, they get excited: "Maybe tonight's the night." That occasional "pay out" is enough to maintain the addiction. Attention seeking children respond in much the same way, a single "pay out" just once a week is enough to keep them at it.

So, if you decide to try ignore certain behaviours, you need to be aware that you have to be prepared for the long haul. Its a matter of months, not days. And both parents need to be consistent.

2. Children choose the worst possible time.

Children don't come to annoy you when you're full of the joys of spring, tra-la tra-la, and bursting with energy. Oh no. They wait till you're on your knees. Friday night after a hard week at work. The wrong time of the month. You're in the kitchen and the phone's ringing. The dog's barking. The baby's been sick. The window cleaner's knocking on the back door. The insurance man's at the front door. You're bending down with a tray of hot fat to go in the oven and you don't know whether you're coming or going. That's the moment they choose. Its not that they're evil (although you may

think that at the time). It's just that they know from experience that that's when you're most likely to respond. Children don't sit down and maliciously work this out, they just stumble over it. And it's very effective. The attention might be negative, but it's still attention.

So, if you decide you're going to try ignore certain behaviours, remember that the most important time is when you are least able to do it.

3. Children choose your most vulnerable points.

Children experiment. They try silly noises. If no response is forthcoming they drop this. Then they fidget. If there's no reaction they move on to something else. They try nose picking. We don't mind, so that one's abandoned also. They turn to sniffing, and we shout "How many times have I told you to use a hankie and blow your nose, it's driving me demented." So that's the one they go for: the one that really irritates, the one we find it hardest to ignore, as **Mr Warner** found.

Mr Warner was a taxi driver. He was very careful to be on time, he hated to be late. **Floyd**, age 12, was constantly late for school. This irritated dad intensely, but it brought Floyd massive amounts of attention.

Children aren't monsters, they just learn this trick. We are all vulnerable. We all have our sore points. And children focus in on these, because we give the game away so easily. Here's an example from a friend, in his own words:

"My son went through a phase of not

eating. My partner was worried to death. It was a vulnerable spot for her. The more she complained, the less the lad ate. I said "Let me handle it ... If you don't want your tea, it's in the bin. You can starve." It wasn't a weak spot for me.

"A little while later, however, the tables were turned. My son started talking in a babyish voice. It got right under my skin. To this day I don't know why, it just irritated the hell out of me. My partner didn't turn a hair. It wasn't a vulnerable spot for her."

So, if you plan to ignore, remember that it's the hardest things to ignore which are the most important to ignore.

ACTIVITY.

Try completing the table on page 28. Be honest with yourself and with your partner, if you have one. Make a list of all the annoying things your child does. The tiny things that irritate you intensely, as well as the big things. Ask your partner to add to the list.

Now, decide which of these could be ignored (even though it is going to be difficult). Think mainly about the small but incredibly tormenting actions, those that are not dangerous but just torture you. You can't ignore breaking a window, but you could ignore sniffing for instance.

I've given one or two as examples to help you start. The list will be different for every family and every family has their own standards and their own breaking points. There are no right or wrong answers, your views will be different to mine. That's O.K., as long

as you come to some agreement and stick to it. And keep it up.

But does it work? It's driving me crazy!

First, it takes time. Longer than you think.

Second, it's only part of the approach. The ignoring must go hand in hand with other tactics. On its own it will not work. Certain things you can not and should not ignore: if he dangles the baby out of the window, you can't ignore that. That's where punishment comes in. And that's extremely difficult to do effectively as well. We'll come to this in chapter 7.

Third, parents often think they're ignoring, but after considering their behaviour in detail, find that, in reality, they aren't. In our family therapy sessions we always have follow-up interviews because these ideas which sound so easy are very difficult to carry out in practice. One parent might find the ignoring almost impossible, another might find the punishments distressing. Both partners may be missing out on praise.

The next chapter examines a few examples of recent cases. For these I have focused mainly on the follow-up interviews where we trouble-shoot the hiccups encountered in trying to follow a programme which involves ignoring. For more detailed examples of the range of kind of problems encountered in the initial interviews, readers are advised to glance at the longer case studies collected together in the appendix.

Irritating behaviours	Are these serious or life threatening?	Could we ignore them for months and months?
examples: Nose picking Silly noises	No	Yes
Burping	No	Yes
Fidgeting	No	Yes
Stealing	Yes	No
Lighting matches	Yes	No
your own ideas:		

Chapter 6

Trouble-shooting ignoring

From long experience, ignoring is often the most difficult part of the programme to carry out effectively. We have to examine in great detail exactly what parents mean by ignoring. It might appear straightforward. It's far from it. Ignoring is not just "sending to Coventry" and totally ignoring everything the child does all day long. Selective ignoring is the essence.

1. Making a sensible choice of what to ignore sounds easy. But it isn't. We may start off deciding to ignore a particular misbehaviour, then find after a while, that we just can't. There is no need for guilt here, just a quiet change of plan.

With regard to ignoring, one mum said she had been making progress, but some aspects of her 13 year old's antics had been getting to her. As one instance of trying to ignore his irritating behaviour, she described how she had been saying to her son, regarding his music, "Turn it down" rather than "Turn it bloody off." We talked about this not really being an example of ignoring. Even though mum had toned her comments down, she was still responding.

The lad had also been kicking the lamp with his feet, and mum said she could not ignore this. She said "I lost it" i.e. she had become very angry with him. We discussed again in more detail the sort of things the parents would be better to concentrate on ignoring, those more minor, irritating behaviours such as his fidgeting.

2. Parents find some children almost impossible to ignore. **Mrs Brookes**, for instance, recalled how **Ewan**, age 7, was so demanding "He takes up your individual space till you agree to whatever he is asking for. You can't even go to the toilet." The secret is to concentrate on one or two areas where you just might succeed. This boosts your confidence, and the child begins to read the message.

3. Deciding exactly how to go about the business of ignoring isn't simple either. You may try to show no response, but still give the game away through body language: the expression on your face, the tension in your hands. Try to imagine yourself on video. What clues would stand out that you had been irritated? Can you dampen these down?

Getting everyone on board is a must. **Ms Watson** explained about her approach to **Melinda** age 12: "I'm thinking to myself all the time, don't change your expression. I told grandma, don't screw your eyes up or grit your teeth"

4. A common problem is the basic one of forgetting to ignore. We set off with good intentions for a few days, then just forget to keep it up. Again, no need for guilt here, just a gentle return to square one and start again.

5. Often one partner will be better at "switching off" than another, and all adults differ on what annoys them. The next family clearly underlines this problem:

Marvin James (age 6). With regard to ignoring, mum said she had found this easy but dad hadn't. Now there was a new problem "He sits and clears his throat." This didn't upset Mrs James but dad said "It grinds on me." Mr James agreed to try to ignore this but said he would find it extremely difficult.

6. As with Marvin above, new irritating behaviours often appear:

Ian McKenzie (age 5). Ian was very attention seeking at home and school. We discussed the sort of approaches to adopt, at our first interview. At the follow-up, Mr and Mrs McKenzie said they had been ignoring some of Ian's little irritating habits such as nail-biting, however, others had appeared, such as a twitch and a cough. They agreed to continue with the techniques, to ignore these new attention seeking behaviours which had developed, and boost the praise he was receiving.

I get the message. Ignoring is important. But is that the key to it? Is that all we have to do?

No, of course not. For more serious matters it is perfectly possible to use, for instance, problem solving and conflict resolution (see Thomas Gordon's books in the further reading section). But sometimes certain behaviours seem to need firm handling, some kind of consequence has to follow. Now, admittedly, "punishment" is a concept with ugly associations of using red-hot tongs and head chopping-off, but we find most parents try to use some form of punishment, discipline, sanctions, consequences - call it what you will - at some time. To keep matters simple we'll just stick to the word punishment, although it is a term with lots of unpleasant side-meanings. Punishment can be part of a loving approach, it does not have to be cold and cruel.

The secret with punishment is to be low-key but effective. And that's much harder than it sounds, as we'll see in the next chapter.

Chapter 7

Punishment

We are still dealing with only one half of the approach in this chapter, one "blade" of the scissors if you like: what to do about misbehaviour. In the last two chapters we considered in depth how to ignore the minor annoyances, to cut down on the attention given to them. Certain behaviours push us to the limit, however, particularly if they are dangerous or destructive or violent. We may finally decide that some form of punishment is called for. Unfortunately this is also difficult to carry out effectively.

No one likes to punish children, so what do we do? We make threats. The child does it again, so we make another threat and put off the punishment. The child then does it again. We become more annoyed, make more threats (and give masses of attention) and put off the punishment again.

So it goes on, escalating out of control as we continue to feed in attention. Eventually, we become annoyed enough. At that point, our anger carries us over our feelings of guilt about punishment. Then we can carry out the threat. But we end up in the worst of all

possible worlds: a giant punishment and an even worse relationship with the child. To multiply our misery, by the time we act, the punishment has also become worthless. It might have no impact at all. It has been "diluted" by all the attention that came before it.

▶ *See how Keith Frost's mum was trying too hard to be a good mother p.59 and did not want to punish or how George Parker's parents felt guilty about the past p.60 and avoided punishing. The problem can be even greater with parents of children with disabilities, see for example Sandra Telfer p.86*

If we are going to attempt to use punishment there is only one way to use it effectively. However, parents usually find this very hard to do. What is needed is to give the punishment early. This way we find a small punishment may be all that is necessary "to nip the problem in the bud." The difficulty is, however, we have to punish the child almost as soon as he starts misbehaving. One warning, then carry it out.

Parents who try this often come back to follow-up interviews and say that, to begin with, they felt cold and calculating. They hated it. Yet when we inspect the situation closely we find that they have, in fact, actually started using much less severe punishments than they had been used to. And they are being more effective, without lots of angry nagging.

So you're saying I can't even get the punishments right. Am I just a total failure as a parent?

No. The problem arises because *you're trying too hard to be a good parent*. By putting off the evil hour, matters spiral out of control. Just to emphasise earlier comments, the punishment, when it finally comes, has to be massive, and even then may not work. Meanwhile, the children enjoy all the attention that is created.

You're not trying to tell me she likes being punished!

No. But what she does like is all the attention surrounding it. The punishment is a small price to pay if you're desperate for attention. Often parents say the punishments are ineffective anyhow: "She's just laughing at me."

We can become accustomed to punishing in a humane but effective manner, even though it hurts us more than the child. One warning, then carry out the threat. It's what we do that counts, not what we say.

There's a whole range of punishments to use. Try to make the punishment fit the crime, that is, try to find natural consequences: "You didn't put your games kit out to wash, so no football for you today, young man." These usually come across as fairer in the long run than arbitrary punishments desperately dreamt up on the spot. Some parents believe in a smack. Many more say it seems to have no impact. Try some of these instead:

No "Top of the Pops" tonight. You're staying in now. Bed! No ice-cream today. Zara can't come in to play with you. No trip to granny's tonight. The sweets are going in the bin. If you can't share the train with Salim, it's going in the cupboard. Go to your room for ten minutes.

ACTIVITY

Make a list of the punishments you use now. Try to judge how effective they are. Be honest, do you always carry out your threats? Do you end up annoyed or do you stay calm? What other punishments could you try?

I've given one or two examples to kick off with. You might not agree with them, that's O.K. Again, there are no right or wrong answers. Every family is different. Every situation is different.

It may sometimes be useful to think of having a parent's strike, if teenagers for instance, abuse their privileges. Why should you iron someone's clothes if they're being awful? Parents have rights as well. Ideally what we want is a home where both parents and children respect each others rights.

Mis-behaviour	Punishment I use now	Is it effective?	Do I always carry it out?	Do I stay calm?	What else Could I do?
Painting on walls	Shout	No	Usually	No	Put paints away
Stealing	Tell off	No	No	No	Stop pocket Money
Fighting	Smack	No	Sometimes	No	Sent to room for ten minutes

But she'll hate me

Parents often worry that their children will stop loving them if they are firm with them. Actually the opposite occurs. We find that the relationship gradually starts to improve as we find more things to be pleased about and spend less time in lengthy, nagging angry punishment.

▶ see for instance Andy West p.69 or John Utting p.81.

Mrs Nugent recounted her style of discipline with Lucy age 12: "I shout, keep her in, talk to her, make threats" all to no avail. After our first interview Mrs Nugent began to be much more assertive. She had noticed with her new partner, who was quite firm: "he gets more respect." When Lucy threatened to run away, mum said "I'll help you pack." Mrs Nugent went on to say, "Our relationship has improved. We chat. She sits next to me and gives me a cuddle."

It seems very important to put across the message that we are only punishing the behaviour, not the child. We can do this by saying, for example, "That was a naughty thing to do", rather than "You are a naughty boy." The difference is tiny, but vital.

It's usually safest to keep matters short and to the point. At the risk of giving too much attention, you might occasionally want to add (in a sincere voice or it won't cut the mustard) something like: "I still love you, but I'm going to have to punish you. Parents are magic, they can do that. I still love you, but you're going to your room."

Of course, effective punishment is easier said than done. We'll examine some samples of the problems parents encountered in the next chapter on trouble-shooting. For more detailed discussions there are the longer case studies in the appendix.

Chapter 8

Trouble-shooting punishment

Some parents find tightening up on discipline quite easy to do. Many don't, however.

1. If there have been long-standing disagreements on discipline it may take months to come to a compromise. As **Mrs Young** explained about her 12 year old son **Duane**:

> "Dad sent him to his room, then he went to work. Duane came downstairs and asked to put his Play-Station on. I walked away. I let him get away with it. I know I shouldn't, but the baby was screaming and the other two were arguing. I'm a soft touch. I feel sorry for Duane confined to his room."

Fay Arnett (age 13) had two parents who disagreed over discipline. At our follow-up interview, Mrs Arnett said dad had followed most of the programme, but there were some important gaps. Mum said she had become much firmer and Fay was "not getting a penny if she was naughty." If she came in late, mum stopped her pocket-money and told her sister and father not to give her any. Mrs Arnett felt mean about this, but stuck to it. Mum had noticed, however, on some

occasions when she told Fay off, dad had then gone to pet her up. She said in some ways Mr Arnett was "soft." However, she said, "If we argue over Fay, there will be more problems."

2. Punishing there and then is better than storing it up, particularly if that means dumping it on the other partner later, as **Mr Ingram** explained about 5 year old **Lee**:

> "Lee just laughs at his mum. But I feel terrible. I come in from work, smack Lee and send him to bed."

3. Starting to tighten up, however, can unleash a whirlwind. Bob Norton's parents recounted at our follow-up "We had six weeks of hell. Bob had even been violent to his favourite uncle, kicking him and drawing blood." Bob was age 5.

Ms Watson, a single parent, described how she began to tackle **Melinda**, age 12:

> "There was something I wanted to watch on TV. Melinda was pushing books in my face, constantly talking

to me and banging around. So, when Emmerdale started, which she wanted to watch, I said the telly's going off for 10 minutes. She hit the roof. She went on for an hour and a half, screaming, running back and forth. She got herself so upset in the end she went into the kitchen and made herself sick."

When we first started the programme Ms Watson quickly went over-board. She grounded Melinda for a month, then she had nothing left to use. We agreed to keep the punishments small and day by day.

4. Learning to use small, effective punishment immediately is crucial. **Mrs Carver** described how she and her new boy friend handled **Nelson**, age 7: "If you touch the keyboard again you'll go to your room for ten minutes. Any problems and its an extra ten minutes. And if you slam the door you're in bed."

5. The rest of the family may need to get involved. **Mrs Dubois** explained with regard to **Ben** age 5:

"He was playing my mother up against me and vice versa. We had a talk. Granny now keeps tight-lipped. I sent him to bed for hitting a friend. The whole thing was so upsetting. But the first one or two times I punished him he was so much nicer. I realised I had won."

6. Very attention seeking children can drive a wedge between adults. **Mrs Thompson** explained how **Edward** age 6 was so demanding "I couldn't go for a pee." He was very jealous of her new boy friend and would push in between

them. She said "In his eyes I'm his and only his."

Mrs Fairlamb, a single parent, described how she had been, in her own words, "on the verge of a nervous breakdown" over **Tim**, age 12.

"In the morning he takes half an hour to get dressed. He just sits there sucking his thumb. I can't take him out anywhere, it's as if he can't walk properly. But he only does it when there's someone else there watching. His legs are up in the air and his arms are everywhere. The more you tell him, the more he does it. I'm fed up shouting and slapping his backside. Wherever we are he shows me up something terrible. Its unbelievable. When he was so naughty his grandma wouldn't have him. I told him not to touch the matches, he went straight to his room with a candle and shut the door and lit it.

"Now his sister is starting to follow suit. When there's a knock at the front door you've seen nothing like it, there's a fight. It's humiliating. I can't have friends in the house. I love Tim to death but I'm not going to put up with it any longer. I started seeing someone. He was really good with the kids, helped Tim with his bike. But he couldn't stand the pressure. We broke up. Now I can't leave Tim behind, and I can't take him anywhere. I can't meet anyone. I'm stuck in the house 99% of the time.

"He screams and shouts at bedtime. He wets the bed every night. He's lost all his treats. I'm screaming at him but he's used to that now. He gets loads of love and cuddles, if I haven't given any it's for a good reason."

As well as agreeing to ignore and praise Tim more, Mrs Fairlamb agreed to try short, early punishment. At the follow-up interview she was surprised to relate, "I'm a lot stronger than Tim. Now he knows I mean no." In the past she had tended to let him get away with things, then over-react. Lately he had begun to accept his punishment "We're making progress. I tell him once."

7. A main barrier is the emotional aspect. Parents may just find punishment upsetting, as **Mrs Valentine**, mother of **Jasmine** age 9, explains:

Six weeks after our discussions, parents observed that changes at home had taken longer than they expected. Jasmine had "rebelled" at first.

With regard to punishment, Mrs Valentine said she had grounded Jasmine, taken sweets away from her and sent her to her room. Mum noted, "It upsets me" although she had carried on with the punishment, and agreed it was important "to be cruel to be kind." Mum emphasised, however, that being firmer had not spoiled her relationship with Jasmine, in fact it had improved: "we talk more."

Mrs Valentine said her approach was low-key but "firm and authoritative." She found she was nagging and complaining a lot less. We discussed how both parents could try to work more as a team so that Jasmine only had one set of rules to follow.

8. Sometimes parents have a sudden "breakthrough" and can see the situation is a new light, as with **Ian McKenzie** (age 5).

At the follow-up interview parents said, "He is still stubborn and defiant and tries it on but we don't give a second chance." Mrs McKenzie went on to say, "It's hard for us to do it." She had noticed on holiday that a friend had been very strict with Ian, she hadn't had time "to mess about." Mum said, "It was quite a lesson to me." She said at mealtimes in the camp, if Ian didn't eat, dinners were thrown in the bin and there was no pudding. This had been an important learning experience for mum.

9. The actual details of how the punishment is carried out may need to be put under the microscope, as with **Marvin James** (age 6).

Mr and Mrs James had been firm with punishment and had been sending Marvin to his room, but this had "turned into a bit of a game." Marvin would come out of his room, wanting to go to the toilet, and then he was back in again asking to come out. However, parents agreed to try to interact with him as little possible when he was in his room, to set a short fixed time, and also to employ other forms of punishment. And, most vitally, to increase praise at other times.

Parents said they were also working more as a team, Mrs James in particular had sharpened up, "I'm not as bad as I was, I'm starting to put my foot down a lot more." But she said, "Sometimes I just forget myself, it's as easy just to give in."

10. Arguing is a disaster zone. We'll meet **Tony Raynor** again later, for the present, it is important to note simply that, instead of mum having an organised approach to discipline, she and Tony would "argue like brother and sister."

Now, picking a calm moment to discuss conflicts, the rules of the house and what is reasonable behaviour and reasonable punishment, is perfectly sensible and fair. Arguing the toss with a screaming seven year old about what should happen when he's just broken a window, is doomed to failure. If you argue, you've already lost. Even if you win the argument, you've lost, because you shouldn't be arguing with a seven year old in the first place.

Unfortunately, if ignoring and punishing is all we do, *the approach will not work*. By tackling misbehaviour this way what we are doing, in effect, is making sure that we do not give the child any attention at all for it. But remember, the child is desperate for attention. If we simply cut back on the amount we give for misbehaviour, he will be starving for attention. He will be forced to re-double his efforts. Children can always find ways of turning the screws when they need to, so that in the end we are forced to respond.

So, we now have to make absolutely sure the child can get attention, but get it "legally", on our terms. And that's where the other blade of the scissors comes in, the part which is often missed, what we do about the child's *good* behaviour. The skill is to catch him doing something we value. Then to go over to him when we decide to, not wait until he misbehaves and become sucked into giving him attention whether we like it or not. We have to *"catch him being good."*

We will turn to this more closely, in the next chapter, the part that's often missed out, the second "blade" of the approach: what we do about the good behaviour.

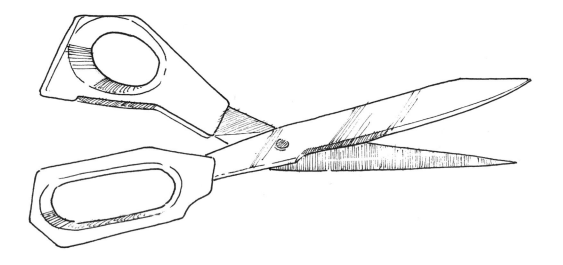

37

Chapter 9

Good behaviour

We tend to take good behaviour very much for granted. Usually, if we say anything at all it will be one or two words in a fairly matter of fact way: "Good lad", "Well done", "Thanks." That's not enough. The child needs masses of attention. Fill her up with praise. She'll soak it up like a sponge. Spend time with her, show that you are pleased with her. Become involved in what she is doing. Involve her in what you are doing. Stand close to her, give her a cuddle. Go over to her when she's reading or playing quietly with her brother.

Catch her being good. Don't wait till she drags you over by misbehaving. Go to her when you don't have to. It will feel funny at first but it will soon start to feel more normal. Don't think to yourself: "They're quiet now, I'd better let sleeping dogs lie." That might be all right for dogs, it's fatal with kids.

So, when Mary hangs her coat up and Sanjay plays with Kim without fighting and Nazmin hands her sweets round and Paul washes the dishes...

"...and you can keep your b*** bread"**

Praise is our strongest weapon. Unfortunately we don't use it enough. It lies about like a rusty sword. Thinking about the impact of praise on ourselves helps to underline the power of praise for children. Praise can even change our own behaviour, as the following story illustrates.

Imagine a situation where a new neighbour has just moved in next door. You hear on the grapevine that she's ill, so you call in on your way to the shops and she says that she'd like you to buy her a loaf of bread. On your way back from the shops you go to her house. Imagine she takes the bread off you and slams the door in your face. You'd probably think twice about calling again.

Now imagine that, when you call with the bread, she says "I'm ever so grateful I've got a neighbour like you. I was worried to death about how I'd make the kids' sandwiches up and we've got no toast for breakfast." More than likely you'd say, "I'll pop in again tomorrow on my way to the shops and see if there's anything else you want."

So your behaviour has switched right round, from refusing to go ever again, to volunteering to go. What made the dramatic difference? A few words of praise. Not that you were angling for it, nevertheless it had a powerful impact on your behaviour. Think how much more powerful it can be with a child. And we don't use it.

▶ *See for instance in the long case studies in the appendix, how George Parker's parents and teacher's had to work at remembering "to catch him being good" p.60 and how Peter Hart's parents found it difficult to give praise p.83. See also how rewards after a long delay were not very helpful to Michael Burdon p.67. Other shorter examples of the problems with praise are outlined later in this chapter.*

Praise in more detail.

Unfortunately, giving praise, appreciation, recognition, call it what you like, is not easy. As with the other parts of the method we need to practise and think about how we are going to praise. It may feel odd and insincere to begin with, gradually, however, it will begin to seem more natural.

- We need to feed in lots of attention. We have to say lots of words and put lots of feeling in to them. The expression on your face has to show pleasure. Give him a cuddle (I know at least one 6ft.2in. hulk who still likes his cuddles).

- There are ways to boost the impact. Here's one we call "Three bites at the cherry":

Dad, praise Ravi for helping you. There's one bite at the cherry. When mum comes in, tell her about it, but make sure Ravi can overhear you saying it. He'll be listening. There's two bites at the cherry. Then mum can go on to praise Ravi for helping his dad. That way he gets three bites at the cherry for one piece of good behaviour.

- Try talking to each other outside Marie's bedroom saying what a smashing lass she's been. She'll be "all ears." Blu-tack a note to her door saying she's gorgeous. Slip a letter under Wayne's door saying that he's "a premier league kid." Ring him up from work just to remind him how pleased you are.

- Make sure other rewards are available also. She is allowed to stay up late or ring grandma or have her friends in or choose her favourite TV programme ... The possibilities are endless. There are lots more examples to try out later. But beware, what is a reward for one child might not be for another. The reward has to be tailored to suit the individual.

- Don't aim to spend a fortune. David Beckham and Posh Spice bought a £45,000 car for their baby. I'm not sure, at nine months old, how well the child would be able to walk, let alone drive. What counts isn't the size of the reward. The most important thing is often just the fact that you're doing something together. You're giving your attention, sharing some time together when you aren't nagging.

- Remember, this is not bribery or "manipulation" for devious ends. This is simply us trying to return to what used to come easily when they were younger: showing children our appreciation for what we all value, the pleasing, positive side of their behaviour. It is good practice, however, not to look as if you are trying to "bribe" or beg or wheedle good behaviour out of them. Rather than saying at the start "If you tidy up, I'll pay you", try to get in the habit of saying after the event: "You've done a lovely job, I'm very proud of you."

Parents sometimes worry that praise will lead to problems. A quote from some very experienced therapists sums up the position perfectly:

If there are any examples of children who have developed behaviour problems as a result of receiving too much praise, we've not heard of them. Children are not spoilt by praise, nor does praise train them to work only for external approval or rewards. In fact, the opposite is true. Children who are motivated only for external approval and attention, tend to be those who have received little praise or reinforcement from adults. As a result, their self-esteem is so low that they are always seeking others' approval, or they demand a reward before complying with requests. On the other hand, children who are frequently praised by their parents, develop increased self-esteem. This positive self-esteem eventually makes them less dependent on approval from adults, and external rewards (see Webster-Stratton and Herbert 1994 p. 252, in further reading section).

To sum up

We cut down the attention we give to misbehaviour, as explained in chapters 5 to 8. At the same time we boost the amount of attention we give for acceptable behaviour. If the child needs attention, he has to swing round and begin to produce more of the acceptable behaviours.

Some ideas for additional rewards

Praise and your individual attention are the best strategies. However, when manners have been very difficult for a long period, extra rewards may need to be used. The following list may give some ideas but, it is vital to note that, what is a reward for one child may not be a reward for another. Check it out with your child before you start. But always remember. Praise is your most powerful aid. Don't miss it out.

These extra rewards should never take the place of praise. Do not come to rely on them. Emphasise the impact of your praise as much as you can. Even if she seems not to like it, deep down she needs it. It may just take some getting used to.

▸ see *the case study of Peter Hart p.83.*

The saddest children are those who have had very little praise but have had a great deal of punishment or criticism. They may lack the confidence to accept praise and may throw it back at their parents by more misbehaviour. That's not an argument for giving up, however, but an even stronger case for carrying on.

Sometimes we need to actively search for things to praise, to create opportunities to show appreciation. If necessary this can be done in a slightly artificial way to begin with, by finding little jobs to do around the house. This is not to make your child a slave, but to break into the vicious cycle of only having negative things to comment on.

List of additional rewards*

Entertainments
Let her choose the TV programmes on Saturday night.
Let her choose the video on Saturday night.
Video games/ computer games / time on the internet.
Trip to the cinema.
Trip to the theatre.
Trip to the pantomime.
Football match (if you can get a ticket).
Speedway.
Motorcycle scrambles.
Cricket match / Rugby match / Ice Hockey match.

Sports and Games
Playing cards.
Playing "Who wants to be a millionaire."
Playing football, with other children or parents.
Swimming, with or without parents.
Dry ski-slope.
Indoor tennis / Fitness room.
Hiking / Fishing.
Ice Skating / Golf.
Indoor football.
Board games, like chess, Monopoly etc.
Computer games.

Music, Arts, Crafts and Clubs
Playing a musical instrument.
Singing, Dancing, Art classes.
Working with wood, clay, tools etc / Gardening.
Joining Scouts, Cubs, Brownies, Woodcraft folk etc.
Cycling club / Sports club.
Running club / Karate club.

Trips
Ride in the car.
Go to work with parents.
Visiting grandparents or Auntie Jean.
Trip to beach.
Visiting a friend.
Visit to museum to see a special exhibition.
Going for a walk in the park.
Trip to the Roman remains.

Trip to a pleasure park.
Trip to an outdoor theme park or old industrial heritage site.
Trip to the Airport.
Return trip on the train to nearby town.
Longest ever bus trip from one end of the route to the other.
Going all the way round on the Metro/ Tube/ Tram.
Trips across the river on the ferry.
Trip up the river on a boat.
Trip to the ice rink or the Megabowl.
Going camping / Wildlife park.
Picnic along the river / Trip to a local beauty spot by bike.
Local museum / Speedway/Visit to a city farm.

Fashion, Food and Toys etc.
New clothes / Special haircut.
Makeup etc / A special toy. (Caution – these can be ruinously expensive.)

Other activities in the house
Having friends in / Going to a friend's house.
Having friends to stay overnight.
Staying at a friend's house / Staying up past bed-time.
Earning extra pocket-money / Having a pet.
Having a party at home.
Getting all your friends in the paddling pool.
Going to a party.
Choice of take-away food on Saturday night.
Sleeping out in the garden in a tent.

*Adapted from La Vigna and Donnellon (1986) in further reading section

We see on page 44 how one family reminded themselves what to praise their six year old son Paul for. They made up a list of all the nice things Paul could do round the house to be helpful. The list was full of clear, concrete behaviours not vague "fuzzies" such as "behave well."

ACTIVITY

Think of all the little jobs your child could do around the house. Include in the list those he already does. This gives you a good starting point of things to praise immediately. Try asking your child what he thinks he should be noticed for, you may be surprised. One boy commented "I'm always nice to dad first thing in the morning, but he's too grumpy to bother."

Then draw up a list of all the possible rewards you could use, on top of your praise and attention. Again, check this out with the child.

Paul's "Can Do" List

Paul can play quietly with Sanjay for 10 minutes.
Paul can get ready himself.
Paul can get washed on his own.
Paul can wash and dry the dishes on his own.
Paul can put his pyjamas on.
Paul can comb his hair.
Paul can run the bath and wash his hair.
Paul can clean his teeth.
Paul can put away his toys.
Paul can make himself a bread and butter sandwich.
Paul can wash his bike alone.
Paul can help to dust and polish the furniture.
Paul can help to tidy the cupboards out.
Paul can close his curtains in his room.
Paul can help his mum with the vegetables for the dinner.
Paul can help mum clean the backyard.
Paul can help mum with the ironing.
Paul can help with the washing and start the washing-machine.
Paul can help to clean the windows.
Paul can set the table.
Paul can pull his quilt over in the morning.
Paul can run a message to the corner shop.
Paul can choose his own books in the library.
Paul can play quietly with his Lego for ten minutes.
Paul can feed pussy-cat Fluff.

Things I could praise	Extra rewards to try, on top of praise

Chapter 10

Trouble-shooting praise

1. Simply keeping going, hanging on to your positive image of the child, even through all the storms of running a programme like this is intensely difficult. We saw how **Bob Norton**, who we met earlier, caused his parents six weeks of hell. Mrs Norton, recalled, however:

> "He looks like an angel when he's asleep. I go and give him a hug and he puts his arms around me. He's not really bad. I can't be negative. That's the only thing that keeps me going. He gives me a hug and says "I love you.""

2. The commonest problem we find in examining parents' feedback, is just not giving enough praise. Simply forgetting. Each day, think back over what you have done. If you can recall only one or two incidents when you managed to praise her in some way, then this will not balance out the negative attention she has been used to. Don't pile blame on yourself, just resolve to try to find more time to praise her tomorrow, more opportunities to create a reason to praise her. **Eva Jones** (age 14) provides a good example:

At the follow-up interview, Mr and Mrs Jones admitted they had not engineered many occasions to praise Eva. Mum said that if Eva went to the shops she would say a quick "Thanks." Mr Jones had been praising her more, however, and Eva had said with pleasure, "My dad's just started speaking to me." We agreed she still needed more praise, particularly from Mrs Jones.

The parents of **Vernon Quinn** age 13, had problems with all the techniques:

> Mum said at the follow-up interview there were signs of improvement, "He plays out more and has more friends." She had been trying to ignore him but "He is the type of child you can't ignore, so I walk out of the room."

> Concerning punishment, Bob (her new partner) had a firm voice, but with regard to her own attempts at punishment "Vernon laughs in my face." She had tried stopping his pocket-money and had stuck to this, even though he became annoyed. She said at first she "felt rotten" then

thought to herself "Why should I feel guilty?" Even so mum said, "He knows he can get me round his little finger." At times Vernon would say, "Don't tell Bob." Mum had been threatening him with Bob, and she agreed, after some discussion that she was turning Bob into "Big Bad Wolf." This also made her even weaker by comparison. She agreed to try to carry out her own punishments.

With regard to praise, however, there had been no jobs for Vernon to do, and on only one or two occasions had Mrs Quinn been able to say, "That's a good boy." It was clear that parents had not found many opportunities to praise him, so we agreed to try again to find lots of little jobs for him to do and make sure he was praised for these.

3. It can take as long to change your habits as it takes to change hers. It may feel strange to begin with as **Mr Oswald** explained about **Jordan** age 6:

"He actually likes getting the praise. We took him shopping for the first time, he helped carry the shopping bags. We never gave him any responsibility till then. He loved the praise. I'm not really a lovey-dovey, grab-you- round the arms type, he's happy with mum doing it."

Over the next few months, Mr Oswald gradually found he could praise Jordan.

Mrs Thompson, a single parent, said at our second interview, about **Edward** age 6, "I'm more tolerant, ignoring the little things, they go over my head." With regard to punishment "I threaten

once and then the punishments are carried out." Mum said, "At first I felt bad, a right old bag ." She had thought to herself, "I can't carry on like this" but she had stuck to her guns.

With regard to praise Mrs Thompson said, "When I first started I was going over the top. I was giving him the love... but he loved it." To begin with, she had found this rather difficult, then she said, "It just comes natural now."

4. Most attention seeking children will leap at the chance to do little jobs around the house. Sometimes persistence may be needed, however, as **Ms Watson** discovered with 12 year old **Melinda**:

"The first time I asked her to wash the dishes it was like I'd chopped her arms off. I explained to her that, if she's helping me, we've got more time together. I usually deliberately keep something downstairs these days, so that she can take it up when she goes. She's doing that quite happily now."

5. One family increased rewards for their child, but he got them willy-nilly, more or less randomly throughout the day. Certainly in the early stages of the programme, you need to tie the rewards very closely to the good behaviours appearing.

6. When using rewards, timing is vital. Try *Grandma's rule*: "First you do your homework, then you can play out." "First you do your dishes, then you watch TV." In this way the child's preferred occupations act as a reward for the less desired activities.

Mrs Simes became a little confused over how to praise **Ray** age 12. He was prone to banging doors. She wanted to praise him when he stopped. She worried that this would encourage him to bang them even more, so that when he stopped banging he would receive the praise, as well as the fun of banging the doors.

We agreed to look at the timing of this. Mrs Simes saw the sense in trying to notice when Ray was walking around quietly, not banging doors, and to praise him then - to get her praise in first, as it were - not to wait till the problem occurred. She commented: "All the time I'm thinking about what he's doing rather than what I'm doing. I'm just responding, not thinking ahead."

7. Even when matters start to settle, however, the problem isn't over. If parents relax and go back to their old ways, the child will follow and slide back to his old ways. **Mr and Mrs Oswald**, parents of Jordan age 6 confessed "We've slowly but surely been slipping into old habits of not praising him."

8. One partner may find praise more difficult, as **Mr and Mrs Valentine** discovered when tackling **Jasmine** age 9.

At the second interview, after six weeks of running the programme, Mr and Mrs Valentine said that now, "She wants more cuddles and she is bringing news home from school." Mr Valentine confessed that he had found it difficult to give praise, but mum had found this easy. Jasmine, in fact, was now approaching dad for praise or a cuddle. Mrs Valentine said, "She's pulling it out of him."

9. Children may look as though they don't want praise. Deep down, however, they do. It may take time to discover this as **David Nichols'** mum found. David was 14, Mrs Nichols had to examine very closely her ignoring, punishing and praising:

Mrs Nichols, a single parent, said at our second interview that she had been ignoring David's "twitching" and leaving his shoes around the house. She had tried to ignore him playing ball in the house which in the end she had to deal with. She said, "Seven out of ten times, you have to intervene." We talked about this as not really being an issue she should try to ignore. Mum said, however, she wanted to give him a chance to stop before she said anything. She felt she wanted to give him "responsibility."

We agreed this was not ignoring in the way we had been discussing, but simply leaving things for a while before she took action. Mum also said that at times when she had been ignoring, she could see herself "making a face." Sometimes she just went into another room. She agreed that going into another room was a good strategy, but making a face when she was trying to ignore, wasn't such a good idea.

Mrs Nichols had, however, tightened up with punishment and was now dealing with things much more firmly saying, "That's it, that's the end of the story" instead of letting matters drag on and drag on. She said she had to do this "Otherwise he knows he's getting attention for ten to fifteen minutes."

Mum had been praising David and giving him rewards such as football stickers. She said that to begin with, things felt artificial, but now, "It just seems to come naturally." She said that when she praised him initially, he gave a "macho response", as if he didn't care. Mrs Nichols agreed, however, "deep down he liked it."

Sam, mum's new boyfriend had had a quiet word with David about one or two issues, and Mrs Nichols agreed that he was in a difficult position and couldn't "come down heavy." David, however, had accepted this reasonable approach, and with regard to the overall management of David's behaviour: "We're going along the same road." There had been rows between the two adults in the past.

Chapters 5 to 10 complete the major elements of the approach. There are, however, a number of additional points which need to be considered. These are tackled in the final chapter.

Chapter 11

Some final points

Even with the best will in the world, it is rare for things to run smoothly in this kind of programme. Some of the more common problems are discussed below. To gain more insight into these, examples of parallel problems in adult life are outlined. These stories are included to put us in the child's shoes, to help us see the child's situation through our own experiences.

(1) Team work

One of the most difficult areas is for both parents to work together as a team. To set the same standards and stick to them. Arguments over approaches to discipline in the home are very easy to stir up.

▶ *See for example the problems brought up with the parents of David Fox p.71 or Philip Gardner p.78.*

Mrs Young, who we met earlier, explained about her and her husband:

"We argue so much about the kids. He thinks I'm sticking up for them. I'm not really - sometimes I am - when he grounds Duane "just like

that." Dad says it before he thinks what he's said. Once he told Duane "you're grounded for the rest of your life."

Harper Cassidy's parents were constantly rowing over Harper age 11. Mrs Cassidy said dad was over the top: "He'll drag him upstairs, belt him, put him to bed, no arguments."

Can you relate this situation of dual standards to your own experience outside of the home? Try to imagine a setting where you're working for two bosses, one of them on the strict side and one on the soft side. Imagine the soft boss brings you a rush job to finish. You do your best, but it needs more time. He says, "Never mind, send it out anyway, the customer's desperate." So you do. And of course the strict boss just happens to pick it up, check who did it and come along to give you hell.

Naturally you're annoyed. You want to tell those two idiots to make their minds up. You're "piggy in the middle." What's more, you still don't know if you were doing right or wrong, it depends who catches you.

The same sort of problem crops up at home. Where is the child if we set different standards? He's "piggy in the middle." He's annoyed. He's confused. He still doesn't know which rules to follow, it depends who catches him.

What often happens, in practice, is that one parent tries to be strict, to make up for the other one being soft. At the same time, the other parent is going all out to be lenient, to make up for the first one being too strict. The parents' approaches move further and further apart. The child drops through the holes in the middle and the parents end up at each other's throats. As one couple said recently, "90% of our arguments are about the kids."

Bob Norton's mum described how, after several weeks of struggling with Bob "I've cut out all the shouting and giving too many chances. I feel more confident that dad's not so quick to punish. We talked about it."

The best plan is to try to make both sets of rules as similar as possible. There is, after all, enough to argue about in a relationship without falling out over the children.

(2) Be careful how you mix 'em.

Criticism usually carries much more impact than praise. We tend to put much more feeling into criticism and it strikes home. Here's a common experience, to put you in your child's shoes.

Imagine that you have made a special anniversary meal for your wife or husband. The first thing they say is, "The peas were like cannonballs." Then they notice you are very upset and try to rescue the situation by

"Is that how you like your peas?"

saying, "Oh, but the steak was lovely, just the way I like it." It's too late. The damage has been done. Nothing can recapture the lost atmosphere.

If on the other hand they start off by saying, "The steak was smashing, the gravy was delicious and the potatoes done just the way I like them, but mind you the peas were on the hard side." Then you would more than likely agree and say, "Yes, I thought they could do with another couple of minutes. Never mind. Have another glass of wine."

In other words, your feelings are not terribly upset when the praise comes first. You can then accept the criticism which follows much more readily.

(3) Things can get worse

Unfortunately, things can get worse before they get better. Your child has always been used to receiving attention through being a nuisance in the past. When you stop giving it, her first reaction may be to become even more of a nuisance, as that always worked up till now. It may be a couple of weeks or more before the message sinks in that the situation has changed.

So if things get worse, don't lose heart. It means that the programme is working. She's started to notice a change!

(4) The big one

When using the approach outlined in this book, it seems best not just to tackle the one big problem everyone is worrying about, the stealing or the truanting or whatever. Instead, what

appears most effective, is to see that problem as just one among many, and tackle them all together.

In this way each "success" with the smaller problems helps us to cope much more calmly with the major issue when it occurs. The child begins to read our more confident body language. And by then the child is also more likely to be starting to fall into the habit of going along with us anyway. Success breeds success.

▸ *See for example, Ann Miller's lack of speech in class p.65; John Utting's delinquency p.81; and Sandra Telfer's refusal to go to school p.86. These were tackled by dealing with the full range of difficulties the children presented, all at once. The "big problem" was handled more successfully by being carried along in the positive atmosphere created by tackling all the small ones.*

(5) Spin-offs

Apart from improvements in the child's actual behaviour we usually also find better relationships at home.

▸ *see for instance Peter Hart p.83 and John Utting p.81*

There may be increased performance at school and greater confidence shown by the child.

▸ *see for example David Fox p.71 and Colin Hurd p.75*

A mixture of praise and a clear set of rules is a great confidence builder.

(6) **ADHD** – Attention deficit hyperactivity disorder

I have the greatest respect for parents living with extremely active children, and the efforts such families have to make to remain on an even keel.

However, that does not do away with the need to inspect this issue very carefully.

ADHD has a confusingly similar name to attention seeking. There is a big difference, however. ADHD children are over-active and impulsive and have poor concentration. The "attention deficit" bit of the label refers to this last characteristic. These are children who find it hard to *pay attention* i.e. they cannot concentrate.

Attention seeking children on the other hand are those who constantly *demand attention*. This is where the confusion sets in.

As we outlined in chapter 1, children can use a thousand and one, bewilderingly different misbehaviours in order to acquire attention. These misbehaviours often include being over-active, impulsive and not concentrating. In other words, some attention seeking children *may appear very much like children with* ADHD. Part of their attention seeking pattern is to be overactive and restless as this brings them lots of attention from their teachers or parents.

▸ see the case study of David Fox p.71 who was initially diagnosed as hyperactive

Even the experts can make mistakes in spotting the difference between ADHD and attention seeking. As a rough rule of thumb, the child with ADHD will find it difficult to settle in most situations. This is held by some researchers to be part of their body's physical make up, a medical condition. The attention seeking child, however, will usually settle if she has someone's undivided attention or is with someone who knows how to give her attention at the right time.

So, if your child is O.K. with granny or Uncle Arthur for instance, or with a very firm but positive and well organised teacher at school, then you may need to question the label of ADHD. But discuss this with your doctor as opinions vary greatly. The reading list at the end of the book goes into more depth on the complications of diagnosing ADHD, and covers material which is both pro- and anti- drug treatment.

At the end of the day, whatever the label, ADHD or attention seeking, the recommended approach to the management of the behaviour problems which are associated with these conditions, may not in fact differ a great deal.

Is it attention seeking or ADHD?

Combining the picture from parents and teachers we begin to understand why this puzzle is so hard to crack. We saw in chapter 1 a sample of the range of behaviours at home which can all be part of an attention seeking pattern. A similar pattern occurs in school. The list below is a collection of the shenanigans several children were getting up to in order to gain attention in class.

Put this list together with the previous list from children at home, and you will begin to see how easy it is to become bemused. Attention seeking can readily masquerade as any childhood problem you care to mention. ADHD, with its impulsivity, poor concentration and over-activity, may be just one of the "conditions" very readily "diagnosed" from collections of behaviours such as these, when the real underlying problem linking all these odd behaviours is simply attention seeking.

Some parents report that medication helps. In some cases children may be taking a drug such as Ritalin, yet certain management issues may still not have been satisfactorily settled.

Melinda Watson whom we met at several points earlier, was diagnosed as ADHD at age 7. You will recall that even such a minor issue as turning her TV off for ten minutes became a major battle when tackled at age 12.

Tony Raynor age 13 had been taking Ritalin for several years and mum was still having serious difficulties with him. Granny gave the game away at one point when we met her by chance. She commented, with regard to her daughter and grandson, "They argue like brother and sister." In other words, Mrs Raynor had not found an effective way to take charge. The drug treatment could not make up for such a difficulty.

A collection of attention seeking behaviours in class.
(The list combines behaviours of a number of children from different schools, in no particular order).

Crawls under desk. Hits chair. Shouts. Flicks ruler. Giggles. Knocks pencil case off desk. Coughs. Throws pencil case. Scribbles on book. Whistles. Makes pig noises. Runs when told to walk. Skips when told to jump. Snatches toys. Pulls models apart. Nips. Kicks. Carries out instructions impulsively and incorrectly. Makes challenging comments. Runs off. Jumps up and down when queuing up. Waves arms about. Blows raspberries. Clicks tongue.

Breaks wind. Stamps feet. Thumps desks. Fiddles with other's belongings. Pulls pictures off the wall. Pokes tops off milk bottles. Pulls down displays. Goes through children's pockets. Throws coats on the floor. Mixes up coats on the pegs. Jumps under the safety rail. Stands at window pulling faces. Asks questions constantly. Late every day. Irritates other children at breaktime. Pinches bottoms. Tells "whoppers." Pretends to have lost dinner-money.

Wears trousers on the wrong way round. Swears. Runs into girls' toilets and drops trousers. Hits the vulnerable children at breaktimes. Disappears at breaktimes. Snorts. Picks nose and puts it in other children's dinner. Tells on other children unfairly. Gets out of seat. Spoils others work. Collects all the equipment together. Wanders round to other tables. Has a nervous laugh. Fidgets. Makes funny noises. Refuses to work. Walks out of class. Lolls about in seat. Argues with teacher. Annoys other children when teachers are around. Runs off and grins all over face.

Takes over other children's games. Pulls a chair out from under a child. Switches machines off. Takes toys from children. Loudly repeats sentences. Removes cushions from chair backs and throws them across the floor. Snatches toys, food or cutlery. Pours own drink into other children's beakers. Obstructs the movement of wheelchairs. Tips children up. Blows on children.

Twists children's fingers. Repeats everything said to him, very quickly. Bobs up and down saying "stop talking" when asked to do something. Pulls the teacher's arm away. Rolls head all over teacher's chest. Trips staff up when carrying objects. Jumps up and down, flaps. Bites own hands. Does "John Cleese" silly walks. Cannot pass an electric socket, light-switch or tap without interfering with them. Shrieks rather than speaks. Fidgets and cannot sit still at story-time. Teases other children. Plays with washing-machines, television sets and gas-cookers.

Shuts self in a room. Screams and has tantrums. Chatters constantly. Runs up and down outside threatening to run away. Runs round the school barefoot. Makes frequent loud burps. Crawls from front to back of the class under the desks and through the children's legs. Licks nose. Drops things, providing excuse to grope around. Laughs at nothing in particular. Loses work sheet. Hums. Bangs on desk with feet.

Puts hand up to ask unnecessary questions. Brings books to show teacher neatness of work constantly. Lies on back with legs in the air banging head on desk. Soils. Comes in late. Has difficulty with reading. Pretends to have convulsions. Whines. Wears long earrings. Lies. Comes without equipment. Pretends to be ill. Hits head with hand.

(7) Definition

There is no simple checklist of behaviours you can use to "diagnose"attention seeking. Almost any behaviour *could* be part of an attention seeking pattern. But it might not. The art is in standing back, not concentrating on individual items of misbehaviour, but trying to see how they all fit together.

As a definition we can say that attention seeking refers to those behaviours which, *through their very irritating nature*, bring a child to the attention of a number of adults in a persistent manner over a lengthy period of time, causing great concern. We would exclude, for instance, the sudden reaction of a child to an upset at home lasting a few weeks. The key is to look inside yourself. Your own sense of intense annoyance usually gives the right answer. For example, we feel sympathy for the child who is "really" ill or upset. The attention seeking child who is whinging or going O.T.T. , evokes a different response from parents: irritation. Making these subtle distinctions when you are under stress, however, is no easy matter.

But to tackle attention seeking we must deal with the *adults'* reactions. There is no individual "cure", no "magic pill", to give the child. It is not a medical condition. Those who wish to read more on the theoretical background can sample "Attention seeking: a practical solution for the classroom", also published by Lucky Duck.

(8) Give yourself a pat on the back

It is important to keep up your own motivation. There is no one else around to do the job. You are your own most valuable asset.

Being a parent is the hardest and most important job in the world. It is also the longest. If you murdered somebody you could be out of prison in ten or twelve years. With children, you've got them for twenty years or more. Sometimes they never leave. It's not surprising we run into problems from time to time.

Keep a little record, day by day or week by week to chart your progress. Remember the pair of scissors: it takes both blades to cut. We have to tackle the good behaviour with as much care as the behaviour which annoys us. You will probably find that you are better at some parts of the approach than others.

Try to review your approach honestly each week or two to see where you need to polish up. But don't pile guilt on your head. It's hard enough to change without beating yourself up at the same time. In one small survey of twenty-eight paediatricians, for instance, these "experts" were found to have had terrible problems with their own children. Three had had children with breath holding attacks, four had struggled with toilet training, eight had had feeding difficulties. Eleven had had sleep problems and thirteen felt their discipline was far from effective. And these were perfectly ordinary children. (Taken from Christopher Green's wonderful book "Toddler Taming", see further reading section).

ACTIVITY : Progress chart

Positive things she has done	Number of times I praised her	Things I ignored	Punishments I carried out calmly

Summary

- The main breakthrough you have to make is inside your own head. To see the pattern behind the bewildering array of misbehaviours your child displays. To see these as attention seeking.

- The next major step is to not heap guilt on yourself and worry about the past. That's water under the bridge. You can't turn the clock back. You did what you felt you had to do, in the way you understood it, with as much strength as you had at that time. Let it go.

- Resolve to start a new approach today. Don't put it off. It won't get any easier.

- You must focus on both "blades" of the approach: deal with the misbehaviour and the good behaviour together. Both of these need a very carefully thought-out strategy.

- Remember that things can get worse. But that means the approach is beginning to work.

- Try to carry out your own trouble-shooting. Scan back over the last few weeks. The commonest stumbling block is lack of praise. But don't forget the team-work needed for punishment and ignoring.

- Don't lose sight of the very positive side of your child. It will start to come through. Attention seeking children are, at the end of the day, some of our most intelligent and engaging people.

- Finally: be kind to yourself.

Appendix

Case studies

The children described in this appendix were drawn from the hundreds of families who sought help from the school psychological service where I was employed a few years ago. I learned a great deal there, working with my late colleague Eric Harvey, a very experienced, highly original and extraordinarily successful, family case worker. The families described below were all interviewed by Eric; they, and I, owe him a great deal.

The schools at that time were mainly organised as infant schools (up to year 2) and juniors (up to year 6), with high schools from year 7. Schools asked for help with (i.e. "referred") these children because of their behaviour in class - behaviour which became recognised as driven by a need to gain attention. Of course we had our "failures." While we can learn much from such failures, I have selected these twelve examples to show what can be achieved with children who are desperate to be the centre of attention; and the confusing difficulties these behaviours cause for parents.

Schools, usually in the shape of the head teacher or special needs coordinator, generally referred children to us, with parents agreement, after a preliminary discussion. These initial discussions were designed to rule out some of the more obvious explanations, and to try out some simple approaches in class. The case notes which follow, concentrate on the most relevant part of the work for this account: the detailed parent interviews. Other aspects of the interventions, such as individual assessments of the children, to rule out learning difficulties for instance, and discussions with the schools about programmes to follow in class, are not included.

In every case described in this appendix, the children had two parents living at home. This is not to deny the difficulties that single parents have, but to underline the importance of the particular problems which arise when two carers adopt different standards. Some examples of single parents, with or without new relationships, are included earlier in the book. This focus on two adults is because arguments between parents are one of the most important barriers to overcome in working with families.

However, I take my hat off to those single mums (and occasionally dads) who can carry out programmes such as this without the emotional support of a partner. The same basic rules apply, it's just that much harder!

Each of the twelve families had one long initial interview then a follow-up interview, usually 6-10 weeks after. In a number of cases, one or two extra discussions were included later. The main ideas of the approach, however, were explored in those first two meetings. The families were then contacted between two to five years after the first interview, for long term follow-up of the effectiveness of the programmes.

Do not feel that you have to read all of these examples. Dip into those that seem interesting to you. I have not given full details of the programme for each family, broadly, however, parents followed the advice given in the earlier sections of this book.

Just to emphasise, the cases have been selected to try to show the range of problems that can occur and that behaviour can change. However, every family's circumstances are different and even so-called "experts" can have difficulties dealing with their own children. So don't lose heart.

CASE STUDIES

Primary age children

(1) **Keith Frost**: A nursery child, age 4, who was displaying aggressive behaviour (p.59).

(2) **George Parker**: Referred when his behaviour began to deteriorate in his infant class, age 6 (p.60).

(3) **Debbie Tait**: She had very poor language and was making slow progress in infant school, age 6 (p.63).

(4) **Ann Miller**: Ann, age 6 had not spoken all year in her year 1 class (p.65).

(5) **Michael Burdon**: At age 7, Michael was referred because of his over-active behaviour in class (p.67).

(6) **Andy West**: A junior school pupil, age 8, who was making very poor progress (p.69).

(7) **David Fox**: His teacher was very worried about his disruptive behaviour in class in top juniors, age 11 (p.71).

Older Children

(8) **Colin Hurd**: He was beginning to show signs of school refusal in his first year in high school, age 12 (p.75).

(9) **Philip Gardner**: He was making poor progress in school and displaying behaviour difficulties at home, age 12 (p.78).

(10) **John Utting**: He was showing early signs of delinquency at age 13 (p.81).

(11) **Peter Hart**: The school were very worried about his tendency to use physical aggression, age 14 (p.83).

(12) **Sandra Telfer**: Age 16, she was attending a school for children with severe learning difficulties. She started refusing to go to school (p.86)

Primary Age Children

(1) **Keith Frost:** *A nursery child age 4, who was displaying aggressive behaviour. Note the irritating tactics he used to get attention such as biting his nails. Note also how his mum had tried too hard to be a "good mum" and had avoided punishments.*

The head of his nursery referred Keith at age four because of great concern about his behaviour. He had a terrible temper and was reported to have "bitten three children in half an hour." There had been a number of tantrums in the nursery. He was seen to be a fairly able boy, to have a good imagination and to be quite happy to chat to adults.

Parent interview

Keith had a normal birth and early childhood and passed his milestones rather quicker than average. He suffered from the ordinary childhood ailments and was not upset when his mother spent a period in hospital after the birth of each of her other children. He was admitted to nursery on a full-time basis when he was just under two and settled in immediately.

Personality

According to Mrs Frost, Keith was a happy, fairly truthful but noisy and

active boy who constantly chattered (this tended to get his mother down). He had, however, a good sense of humour. Unfortunately, as well as being stubborn, defiant and argumentative, he also liked a lot of his own way. He was however not too demanding and would willingly wait to have his wants satisfied.

Keith resented discipline and when checked would indulge in minor temper tantrums. He had a tendency to show off but would often help in the house quite readily with small jobs and enjoyed praise. He was a sensitive child easily reduced to tears and made no effort to hide his feelings. If interested he could display a fair amount of patience and appeared to have confidence in himself. He was neat and quite enjoyed being tidy.

Relationships with brother and sister were rather poor because of his domineering and aggressive behaviour. This was also the case with other children outside the family.

Keith had no food fads but he would suck his thumb. He would also bite his toenails and his fingernails. This habit particularly annoyed his mother who responded by feeding in a great deal of attention. He was quite happy to go to bed early and did not wet the bed and was a calm, restful sleeper. Unfortunately, although he was able to dress himself he always dawdled in the mornings which provoked Mrs Frost to go on and on at him.

Management

Mrs Frost said that she lacked patience. She said that her approach was to "tell and tell" and then go on telling until in desperation she would resort to threats. She rarely, if ever, however carried these threats out. Her husband did not take any hand in disciplining the children.

Discussion

Mrs Frost was quite receptive to suggestions that Keith was creaming off a large share of attention in the house (she had two other children all under school age) through a variety of irritating and annoying behaviour such as biting his nails, dawdling, arguing etc. It appeared that, also, some of his activities in the nursery were equally effective in bringing him to the attention of the nursery staff.

It was clear that Mrs Frost had been trying hard to "be a good mother." She had, quite unnecessarily, been worrying about the children having to go into care if she punished them. This had led her to try to avoid disciplining them at all. Unfortunately, in Keith's case this had meant putting off the matter until it escalated out of all control. By that time she was worried about "going too far" and so she still usually avoided punishing him. Mrs Frost agreed to try small early punishments and to get over her guilt about these.

At the same time Mrs Frost agreed to make a special effort to involve Keith around the house (as he was the oldest) and to praise him. She said she would look for lots of opportunities to give him attention at times such as these, as far as she was able to in her rather busy home. She recognised that these occasions allowed Keith to receive the extra attention he needed. Ignoring his more minor, irritating behaviours, to

cut down on the attention he gained for these, was the final part of the strategy.

Follow-up interview

Seven weeks later Mrs Frost seemed much more relaxed and calm and said that there had been a marked improvement in Keith's behaviour and attitudes at home. He had become more obedient and biddable and he was not so argumentative or as stubborn. As well as becoming a great deal tidier, folding up and putting away his own clothes, he had shown that he could be a good help in the house. Mrs Frost said that she was now emphasising these very positive behaviours by praising him. As a result he had far fewer tantrums and now also appeared to be enjoying much better relationships with his brother and sister.

Mrs Frost had, unfortunately, found it very difficult to ignore his nail biting. He had in fact bitten his nail right down to the skin. She agreed that both she and her husband found this particularly irritating but she would make a further effort to tackle this and be more consistent in ignoring it over a long period.

Over the following months Keith's behaviour gradually settled in the nursery and we did not make any further appointments. Four years later, when we called in for long term follow-up, things were going well at home.

(2) **George Parker:** *Referred when his behaviour began to deteriorate in his infant class, age 6. Note the range of behaviours which brought attention - from being an express train to banging his head and not making progress. Note*

also the problems around his birth which left his mum with a poor relationship with him and feeling guilty.

George was referred at age six because of increasing concern about his behaviour in infant school. He appeared to be of average ability and coping quite well with everyday class work. He was however a solitary child, prone to rushing his work, easily distracted, unpredictable and careless. His behaviour had deteriorated to a marked extent recently and he had begun attacking other children. Although these attacks were not particularly violent, they were persistent and constantly annoying to the other children. The behaviour seemed to occur more openly in the playground than in class. There were indications that George had been upset by his home being renovated but it was felt that this did not explain all of his behaviour over a number of years.

Parent interview

George had a younger sister. Both parents were extremely anxious about his ill treatment of other children and had been looking for explanations. George himself said that he attacked other children "because I'm sick of the house without carpets and that." That was not the whole story however!

Early history

Mrs Parker said that she was fretful, agitated and uncomfortable right throughout George's pregnancy. She had to go to hospital because of high blood pressure before his birth and there was talk of a caesarean which upset her even further. Complications set in during the birth and mother had quite

an unpleasant time. He was small when born and then whisked away because of jaundice and Mrs Parker didn't see him for several days. When at last she did see him she felt "indifferent - I never bonded to him."

Mum revealed that she had suffered from post-natal depression and admitted that George's incessant crying got on her nerves so that she had once "flung him onto the settee." It was only several months later that the depression lifted and Mrs Parker began to enjoy him instead of regarding him as a burden. She did not realise what a common experience this was for mothers. Matters were totally different with the younger girl who had been a joy throughout.

Personality

The two children would not share toys and George would tend to push his sister and exclude her wherever possible. He himself would also "act babyish" which brought irritated reactions from his parents, particularly his dad.

George had always been a "headachy child" according to his mum. He was very active "like an express train" and no ornaments were safe near him. He was very headstrong and disobedient and "deliberately goes on and on" until he "vexed" his mother. She had naturally been very upset by this and had tried to reason with him saying, for instance, "why do you force me to push you away and be annoyed with you when all I really want to do is cuddle you?"

George tended to show off in front of company becoming "rotten and awkward." He would fuss at mealtimes also and this brought a great deal of attention from his mum. Although he seemed a healthy child generally, he often complained of headaches and earaches etc. He told tales. He could be talkative and quite entertaining. Unfortunately his quite reasonable self help skills were taken for granted and not praised. He could also sit quietly, for instance watching TV for a long time "you wouldn't know he was there." This was not singled out for praise either.

As a pre-school child he had taken to banging his head. Complaints about his poking and hurting other children began at nursery. It was reported that he liked the attention of his teachers but could not cope when other children were the centre of attention.

Recently at home he had started bed wetting although he had been dry for many years without any trouble.

Discussion

Mr and Mrs Parker were both extremely anxious and probed for reasons for George's aggression. The parents had a great feeling of guilt after his early illnesses and the difficulties surrounding his birth. Unfortunately this meant that they would often act in irritation and then try to compensate with extra affection. These early difficulties, and perhaps the birth of his sister, could easily have been the triggers for an attention seeking cycle. We did not probe these, however, nor did we look for "medical" explanations for his misbehaviours. We focused on the "here and now", and the parents' approach.

It was clear that George was using a wide range of behaviours to get his parents' attention. All the examples such as having headaches, being very active, "going on and on", showing off, fussing at mealtimes, acting babyish, banging his head, being aggressive with other children and his sister etc. were very effective in provoking immediate and prolonged attention from his parents. They agreed to try to ignore those aspects of his behaviour which could be ignored and to be firm and consistent with those which required some form of punishment.

Instead of focusing on the past it was agreed parents would concentrate on what to do today, and not feel guilty about having to use appropriate small punishments as and when needed. In addition Mr & Mrs Parker agreed to try to find helpful responsible behaviours (which George would in fact quite readily carry out) and to pay particular attention to them. As it turned out, George loved praise.

School behaviour

In class at that time, George was seen to be crawling along the floor to get paper; calling out silly words in the middle of prayers; chatting loudly and in a silly way with his friends; constantly going to the teacher for every little part of his work to be looked at etc. Even though his work was quite adequate he was getting a great deal of teacher time simply by being incompetent in class with his work. After some discussion, his teacher accepted that she had been falling into the trap of taking more notice of him when he was not working because of her concern about wanting him to make progress. She quite happily accepted suggestions of trying to "catch him being good" and praising him then, instead of only going over to him for correction.

Follow-up interview

Mrs Parker was very enthusiastic and excited about the changes in George's behaviour. She had taken on board very well the need for positive attention and praise. Already George was offering to do many more helpful jobs in the house such as hanging up clothes when asked, behaving more pleasantly with his sister, concentrating on writing and colouring, and watching TV programmes for extended periods. Altogether he seemed much more happy and relaxed. This change in itself had dampened down mum's anxiety considerably. She wanted the advice to be repeated so that the points could then become more clear to her husband. He was still inclined to take more notice of George when he was irritating.

For the past few days George's bed had been dry and Mrs Parker had fed in very strong rewards for this. She admitted in the past she would have tended to "rant and rave" and try to push him towards better behaviour, and dry beds. She also admitted that often when she received bad reports from school she had followed this up with punishments such as early bed and withdrawal of love and privileges in the hope of "teaching George a lesson." She now saw quite clearly that this was a fruitless way of trying to change matters. He responded best to more positive attention, at the right times.

Improvements continued for several months. With a change of teacher, however, difficulties began to re-occur. By arranging close contact between home and school, it was possible to provide George with appropriate rewards and incentives (such as working towards a school trip) to tackle these difficulties.

Twelve months later George had not been re-referred and matters appeared to be settled. His mother later informed us at long term follow-up that he had become a more affectionate boy and had said to her, "Thanks mam, for making me better."

(3) **Debbie Tait**: *She had very poor language and was making slow progress in infant school, at age 6. Note her early illnesses which could have been a "trigger" and how dad wanted to keep her as "my little baby." Note also how, instead of concentrating on just one problem (her speech) a whole range of difficulties was tackled.*

Debbie was referred because of concern by her mother and speech therapist about school progress. She suffered from a severe allergy causing sinus and catarrh infections and occasionally slight deafness in one ear. She had a sinus wash and both ears drained the previous year. At school she had developed a great fear of failure and was very withdrawn and unhappy. Debbie had made very little progress with early number and early reading skills despite being of average ability.

During assessment she was panicky about the materials and her speech was more or less unintelligible. Mother had to act as interpreter.

Parent interview

Parents were interviewed and it became clear that at home Debbie was quite assertive, humourous and confident in marked contrast to being withdrawn and lonely at school. She was, however, in some ways very insecure after a number of hospitalisations because of her poor health and the family had tended naturally to focus on her fears and illnesses. At home, however, Debbie could be a "tyrant" with her dad if denied her own way. She even threw her clothes one by one into the road to force him to carry her home when he was trying to insist that she walked. In the end Debbie won. Father tended to refer to her as "my baby girl." He tended to pick her up and treat her as a much younger child because she looked so frail. Very little notice was taken of tasks achieved or displays of maturity. Debbie tended to depend on Ann, her sister, who was quite sensible and responsible. Her mother felt that praising Ann would upset Debbie so she had tended to take Ann's good points for granted.

Management

When it came to discipline at home Debbie could generally joke or talk herself out of trouble and slide out of the consequences of minor misbehaviour. Mum was stricter over major problems however. Debbie was given plenty of rewards but these tended to "come out of the blue" and never dependent on having made an effort to please anyone. She was, for instance, given first choice of bedroom in the new house the family moved to. When they moved in she was also given the choice of wallpaper to encourage her to sleep in the room she had in fact chosen. Debbie had then made other requests for furniture and arrangements in her room, then still ended up sleeping with her parents.

Mrs Tait had tried to set down rules and guidelines for Debbie but she could easily get round these by talking to her dad.

Parents were of the opinion that Debbie's poor speech was a critical factor in her not mixing well with other children. They worried a great deal about her speech.

It was clear in discussion that there was a marked difference in the parents' approach to Debbie. Father was inclined to treat her as a baby and be indulgent. He was quite easily manipulated by her. Mother was much more consistent and less open to her manipulation and this had led to her parents arguing. Debbie was quite able to play one off against the other.

Parents were quite responsive to suggestions about viewing Debbie's difficulties in terms of obtaining attention. They realised the need to be clear about when to give attention. Mr and Mrs Tait readily agreed to praise her more generally, and to try to find lots of little jobs for Debbie to carry out so that they had extra excuses to praise her. Parents also accepted the need to ignore any little irritating habits and to play down her speech difficulties, but to tighten up on discipline. In particular, they resolved to try and work more as a team.

Follow-up interview

At a follow-up interview one month later, the parents said they had modified their approach to Debbie along the lines suggested and she had been "fantastic." Mr Tait had made a greater effort to firm up his approach and as a result Debbie now seemed much more mature and happier in herself. She was much more confident and now accepted "when we say no, we mean no." Debbie was also taking much more interest in her reading both at home and at school and was generally showing much more interest in school overall. Furthermore, at home she would now apologise when she misbehaved.

The parents were "over the moon" with the change in Debbie. Mother confirmed "I'd kept her as a baby too long." Her teachers in school also helped to give her confidence by building up her morale and praising her for improvements in her work. A letter to us from the speech therapist about one month later said :

"I am very pleased to report a sudden improvement in Debbie's phonology (speech sounds). Her speech is now much clearer especially when reading aloud to me from her school reading book. Mr & Mrs Tait appear to be carrying out your suggestions and they are much happier about Debbie generally."

Debbie continued to make progress in school. Mrs Tait asked for her to be given a reading book and Debbie became very keen to read at home. This helped her a great deal, her mum reported some time later at long term follow-up.

(4) **Ann Miller**: *A primary school child, age 6, who had not spoken all year in class. Note how not speaking was very effective in school as a way of obtaining attention but also note that this went hand-in-hand with a number of difficulties which needed to be tackled at home.*

The head of Ann's primary school referred her in year 1. She had some difficulties adjusting in reception class the previous year but towards the end of that year had opened out. During year 1, she had not spoken in class either to teachers or friends.

When seen at the office, outside school, Ann chatted away quite happily. Assessment showed that she was a bright little girl.

Parent interview

Ann had a normal birth and early development. Her sister was born when Ann was 2 years. Ann settled well in play group although she was quiet. In reception class in her primary school she did not speak until about Christmas. She then began to chat quite readily until moving into her new class.

Personality

Ann had always been a somewhat reserved child but happy and truthful with a good sense of humour. However, as well as being extremely noisy and active in the home (which tended to annoy both parents) she was very stubborn and defiant and would often do the opposite of what she was told. She did not demand material things, she showed affection quite readily and had patience but often seemed to lack confidence. Ann would help with little jobs in the house but if not "in the mood" would refuse outright. She also resented discipline.

Ann related well to her sister and could happily occupy herself. She did, however, have the annoying habit of constantly fidgeting. This brought a great deal of attention from her parents. She also tended to dawdle in the mornings. This made mum "go on and on" at her and usually end up dressing her.

Management

Mrs Miller said that she was fairly patient. Her approach to Ann was to tell her a few times before starting to shout and then to make threats. It was only "as a last resort" that she carried out the threats. She admitted that Ann could easily manipulate her.

Mr Miller said that Ann could "soft soap" him to a certain extent also, but she was generally more obedient for him than for his wife. Mrs Miller admitted that at times she had stopped her husband from punishing Ann. Mum said "I tend to think of her as a baby."

Both parents were very concerned about Ann and wanted the best for her. They agreed, however, that she was getting a great deal of attention because of not talking at school and because of her fidgeting and dawdling at home. Furthermore, she was still wetting the bed quite regularly, which again brought a fair amount of negative attention. Mrs Miller had herself tried a "star chart" (i.e. little stars and rewards whenever Ann was dry) to clear up the bed wetting. She had had some temporary success with this. Mum agreed, however, to try the approach again, but with extra rewards and praise for dry beds, at the same time as she tackled all of Ann's difficulties together. A particular emphasis was placed on finding lots of activities around

the house to give Ann positive attention for generally. She "beamed" when praised.

A final area of concern we discussed was Ann's reading. While she was, in fact, making reasonable progress, both parents were very worried and had fallen into the habit of giving her practice sessions at home lasting up to half an hour. These were often stressful for both Ann and her parents. They were very anxious for her to improve and this made them very tense and try too hard to be what they thought of as "teachers." This led to them being very strict and critical rather than seeing the reading session as a fun time like going for a walk or learning to ride a bike. Mr and Mrs Miller agreed to cut these sessions right down and to adopt an approach which made reading much more pleasant for all of them. The approach was given the title "Cuddle and Read."

This "Cuddle and Read" approach involved very short periods (five minutes or so) with Ann sitting on mum's knee, having a cuddle as they enjoyed their time together. Mrs Miller agreed to say nothing about Ann's mistakes but simply to give her the right word and pass on quickly. She continued to praise and cuddle Ann throughout the session, emphasising her success. She encouraged Ann to guess, even when the guesses were "wrong." Mum came to realise that even making a "wrong" guess was better than Ann being so scared of failure she would make no guess at all. She stopped judging the guesses harshly as either right or wrong. She simply concentrated on praising Ann for words she read correctly and having the confidence to try with words she found difficult. Mrs Miller began to see learning to read like learning any skill - something that responded best to praise and encouragement. Her anxiety to be a "good parent" and develop Ann's reading, had, ironically, got in the way of taking a more effective but low key and positive approach.

Follow-up interview

Mrs Miller said that Ann "seems more co-operative - more grown up." She was by then helping in the house more and often volunteered to help, "she's dead keen." She loved the praise which followed. She was also much more obedient. The bed wetting had improved but was still rather erratic.

At the open night at school the previous week, it turned out that Ann had made no improvement at all unfortunately. In mum's opinion "she had them all on a string." From her description it appeared that the Headteacher, the class teacher, the dinner ladies - in fact, everyone - tried to get Ann to speak. Obviously school, without intending to, had been feeding in a great deal of attention over this matter. Mrs Miller herself, however, felt guilty about what she saw as her own mistakes in handling Ann. She did not have a great deal of confidence in herself in any case. We spent some time discussing this area, emphasising that mum's "mistakes" had arisen in fact from trying too hard to be a good parent.

At a further interview one month later, Mr & Mrs Miller reported that Ann was now much more outgoing than she had been. Her confidence was growing and she was going to visit a friend's house. The bed wetting was improving slowly but she was still not talking in class. Again Mrs Miller talked about her own shyness and also her feelings that she had "coddled Ann too much when she was younger."

Another meeting a few weeks later revealed that Ann had finally started talking in class. Her teacher was now complaining that she was, in fact, being rather disruptive with her constant chatter!

During the discussion it also turned out that the younger sister had had speech problems after a convulsion and had seen a speech therapist. It seemed that Ann's lack of speech in class had triggered off, quite naturally, a lot of extra worries for her parents and been a ripe area for obtaining attention.

At a final appointment, six months later, Mrs Miller said, "Things have been great, both at home and at school." Ann seemed much more mature and now accepted discipline without resentment. She would start conversations quite readily with anyone and overall she was "a different little girl."

Ann continued to make progress in class generally, but also with her reading, and had not been re-referred by school three years later at a long term follow-up visit. Her work was up to scratch.

(5) **Michael Burdon**: *An infant school boy, age 7, referred because of his over-active behaviour in class. Note how his foster parents wanted to make up for his past and how his foster mum felt guilty about punishing him.*

Michael, aged seven, had been with foster parents, Mr & Mrs Sanderson for three years. School referred him because of concern about his very over-active behaviour in class. When observed in class he made himself very obvious. He angled to get himself last in line on coming in. He immediately came up with complaints about being banged on the nose. He was out of his seat playing with a ball on an elastic thread which had been banned the day before. Michael was constantly restless and swinging back in his chair, fussing over his pencil which needed sharpening. He was using a very loud voice and chattering constantly with girls at his table.

His teacher had tried giving Michael stars in a progress book to earn prizes. Unfortunately, in six months he had only earned six stars. Although the idea was good the time scale and rate of reward were obviously inappropriate. The standard had been set too high and he was just not receiving enough rewards. The programme was doomed to fail.

Parent interview

Mr & Mrs Sanderson described Michael as an affectionate, friendly child, keen to please and happy to help, never malicious but overactive, argumentative and determined to have his own way. What was particularly annoying was his "dawdling" in the morning and his resistance to going to bed at night. There was also a great deal of aggressive behaviour when visiting relatives. As they lived in an upstairs flat, they had little opportunity to take him out and his play was restricted.

Management at home

Mrs Sanderson admitted to lacking confidence and having to rely on her husband for everything. There had even been a time when she had been afraid to go outside herself. She tended therefore to try not to use her own authority and threatened Michael with Mr Sanderson rather then carry out sanctions herself. This, of course, undermined her authority with Michael even more. Mum generally tried to reason with him and then threaten, and then end up "going on and on" and shouting at him. Mrs Sanderson also "felt guilty" after punishing Michael. She tended to undo the punishments by making up to him afterwards. Mr Sanderson was rather more decisive about the matter.

Discussion

Instead of focusing on Michael's difficult history, which had led him into care (and which encouraged Mrs Sanderson to be lenient "to make up for the past") Mr & Mrs Sanderson were quite happy to begin to consider the here and now. Discussion concentrated on ignoring many of the irritating activities that Michael had displayed such as dawdling. In addition, Mr & Mrs Sanderson were very receptive to ideas about stressing positive approaches as well as accepting suggestions about learning how to praise him and show appreciation much more clearly and readily. They talked about arranging a number of other treats for him such as listening to his favourite video programme, having a game of darts or snooker, taking his bike to the park, going to the beach, listening to a story etc. Finally, both parents agreed that by not working as a team Michael had not learned to follow a consistent set of rules. This prevented them taking an effective approach to his misbehaviour.

Follow-up interview

Mrs Sanderson reported that Michael's behaviour had been much better lately. She had found it possible to tighten up her approach to discipline. She had not, however, as suggested, arranged for Michael to carry out little household tasks in order to have a legitimate and obvious reason for praising him. Even so, there had been a number of areas of improvement, for instance, Michael was now able to play much more happily with her nephew of the same age, and she had had many fewer complaints from school about him. Mum agreed to re-new her efforts to praise him.

Three months later in school, Michael's teacher reported a great improvement in his behaviour. Generally he had not been misbehaving in a way designed to bring himself to the teacher's attention. It was stressed with his teacher to be on the look out for positive behaviour and he agreed to do so. "Good" sessions were coloured in on a class timetable and Michael was given lots of praise.

Several weeks later, some aggressive incidents were reported in the school playground. There were, in addition, some further incidents of wrestling and poking and moving things around in class. It was agreed to arrange a short home-school diary for Mr & Mrs Sanderson to help support his behaviour in school. Parents were in a much stronger position then to build on the greatly improved attitude he showed at home. He was much more responsive to them generally at home at that point. As a consequence, he was also much more responsive to their praise for positive comments about his behaviour in class, recorded in the diary. We agreed that a home-school diary would have had little effect when we first met, as a result of Michael's manner at home at that time.

With this extra support, matters settled and one and a half years later the case had not been re-referred and Mr & Mrs Sanderson were pleased with Michael at home when we made a long term follow-up visit.

(6) **Andy West**: *A junior pupil, age 8, making very poor progress. Note how his parents tended to be lenient with him because of medical difficulties and how he could recall a great deal of attention coming to him through misbehaviour. Note also how his work improved as his behaviour was dealt with.*

Andy was referred by his junior school aged eight because of concern about his academic progress. His teacher said that he would be quite happy to spend all day "doing jobs" and although he was a friendly, cheerful lad, always ready to answer questions and to talk quite readily, he would attend to anything but his own work. He generally never got down to any solid work and would soon switch to something else, whatever the task. Andy's relationships with other children were good but he would tend to misbehave often when the teacher was engaged with other children. When seated at the table he would twist about in his seat, slip on the floor or climb about on his desk. He was constantly restless, tapping with his pencil, shuffling with his feet, changing his position etc. Although not a leader in this behaviour he would often follow other children.

Parent interview

Both parents attended. At eighteen months Andy was in hospital for a few days because of a fractured skull. He was then discharged, largely because of his fretting. At six he was again in hospital for a few days because of a broken arm. He needed to wear spectacles but objected strongly to this. Andy had attended the hearing clinic regularly and it was felt that at some point he would have to have his tonsils and adenoids out.

Pre-school he was a good mixer and settled well at his infant school. He was inclined to cry the first few weeks he was admitted to juniors and although he seemed initially somewhat reluctant he had been attending regularly.

Personality

According to Mrs West, Andy was a happy, carefree, very truthful boy with a good sense of humour. He was inclined, however, to be very noisy and active which tended to irritate both parents. He liked his own way but was not very demanding for material "goodies", however, he was inclined to be very stubborn and argumentative. He resented discipline and when checked invariably claimed that he was being picked on. He was a sensitive lad who was very open with his feelings, but had a tendency to cling to his father. Andy would help in the house and showed a fair amount of patience but tended to lack confidence. Relation-ships with other children were good and he was well able to stick up for himself. He tended to bite his nails which brought a great deal of attention from his mum.

Management

Mr West said that he was in charge of discipline. His approach was to tell Andy once, then threaten a punishment, and then carry out the threats. He said that he was not vulnerable to Andy's manipulative tactics. Mrs West claimed to be patient. She said her approach was to "tell a few times" before resorting to threats which were rarely, if ever, carried out.

Andy

He was in the average ability range but spoke in a slightly immature style, however, he was quite friendly. Andy said that he liked school but not maths. He said he would do a number of jobs in the house and could remember the odd word of praise. He quickly volunteered, however, that he was told off for being noisy, arguing with his brother, being cheeky, biting his nails, being untidy, eating too much etc. In other words through Andy's eyes he could recall a great deal of attention coming for these irritating behaviours. We discussed what would be the most effective approach that parents could adopt in terms of discipline. After some thought he said that fairly firm parents with a "no nonsense" style would in the long run suit him.

Discussion

Mr & Mrs West agreed to try to put Andy's early medical difficulties behind them and to deal with his behaviour now. They readily accepted the need to operate more as a team. They were helped by hearing Andy's views related to them about discipline. They were also somewhat surprised to find out that their praise had not really penetrated but that Andy could recall a great deal of being nagged at. This brought about a long discussion about the need to practice, and be very clear about, praise to increase its impact.

The parents agreed to try this for the next few weeks along with other suggestions about ignoring his nail biting and trying not to argue with him. They said that it would be difficult to be firm with Andy, however. They had tended to be lenient with him because of his medical difficulties and periods in hospital when he was younger.

Follow-up interview

Two months later his school reported that Andy was "no bother in class." He was not showing any difficulties at all "he just sits down and gets on with his work." He appeared to be enjoying attending school and was reluctant to stay away, even when he was feeling off colour. His work rapidly began to improve.

Mrs West said that Andy seemed much happier in himself and she no longer had to nag at him so much. Relationships between them were much happier. She had found it easier than she thought to be firm with him and she and her husband had, after some initial hiccups, agreed that it was better in the long run to act as a team, setting similar standards. In addition, Andy had been quite ready to accept helping in the house and was pleased with the extra affection this brought. The parents had also agreed to stagger bedtimes and pocket money to give his brother a little more status. Andy surprisingly had accepted this quite well.

In view of the progress shown, no further appointments were agreed and three years later Andy was still settled at long term follow-up.

(7) **David Fox**: *His teacher was very worried about his disruptive behaviour in class in top juniors, age 11. Note how early hospital treatment and going into care could have acted as "triggers." Note how mum's emotions showed clearly on her face and how the parents were trapped into arguments between themselves. Also see how his confidence and school work improved as his need for attention was tackled.*

David was referred by his junior school teacher one term after his transfer there from a neighbouring school. His achievements appeared to be about average for his age but his class teacher reported that his behaviour was not acceptable. He was inclined to disrupt the class by calling out, although he was also able to make positive contributions to class discussion. David's writing was appaling and done at record speed and apparently without thought. He made no effort to control his movements when writing. He was very easily distracted and would prefer to have no demands made on the time he spent gazing around the room. David loved to be noticed, however, and also liked to prevent others from working. Although he read fairly well with expression and had a good general knowledge, in general he was capable of only very short lived concentration and effort. He needed constant watching and correction.

Parent interview

Mr & Mrs Fox both attended. David was an only child. He had a normal birth without complications and was a contented baby. He proved, however, extremely difficult to feed but this problem was overcome and he passed his developmental milestones within normal limits.

He had the normal childhood ailments but he was rather prone to bronchitis. At age two year six months his GP prescribed medication because of his "hyperactivity" and he carried on with this until aged four. At four, he spent a couple of days in hospital having his stomach pumped out after taking a great deal of this drug by mistake. At seven he was in hospital for about five days after an operation for an undescended testicle.

Mrs Fox said that when David was six he was admitted to voluntary care when grandparents had great personal difficulties and his parents couldn't cope with these problems as well as David. He was fostered for nine months. His parents complained that they were only allowed to see him for a short period. On his return home, David often compared his parents unfavourably with his foster parents. He commented particularly on material comforts that the foster family had provided. Mr and Mrs Fox had separated on occasions for short periods during this period of great family pressure.

Pre-school David was able to get out and about and proved to be a good mixer. He settled well in playgroup and then nursery and also infant school. Although he liked the school they very quickly complained that he was extremely naughty and disruptive. This continued when he transferred to another Infant School when he went into care.

Shortly after returning to his parents they had to move house and that involved David transferring to his present school. He settled in quickly but then the school began to complain about his disruptive behaviour.

Personality

According to Mr & Mrs Fox, David was not a happy boy. He had a good sense of humour, however, and was honest in the sense that he had never taken anything but he had a tendency to tell lies. As well as always being "on the want" for things and demanding his own way, he was extremely noisy and active. This tended to get both parents down. Furthermore, David was stubborn, defiant and argumentative. While he generally could wait to have his wants met, he was inclined to "go on and on." Both parents usually gave in. David usually resented discipline and when checked or denied his own way would indulge in tantrums in which he would fling things around the bedroom. Generally, however, he would help in the house when told to do so. He received little praise for this, however.

His parents felt that David was an extremely sensitive boy with a tendency to cry easily but usually he would try hard to hide his feelings. He had no patience, a low tolerance of frustration and lacked confidence. He was also very untidy and Mr and Mrs Fox picked up after him. He was usually bad tempered.

Relationships with other children were usually quite good but David tended to play with those four or five years younger than himself. He was unable to stick up for himself with children of his own age.

David was constantly fidgeting which annoyed both parents. He had a good appetite but was rather faddy about his food and his parents usually tried persuasion. When this failed they allowed him to fill up with biscuits and sweets. He had a number of interests but was also a television addict. This brought a great deal of negative attention from the parents. David was a good sleeper but tended to dawdle over his dressing in the morning with the result that the parents were inclined to go on and on at him.

Management

Mr Fox was in charge of discipline. He said that he had little patience and that his approach was to tell the boy several times and then start shouting at him, then finally make threats. He admitted, however, that he rarely carried out his threats and that he was vulnerable to David's manipulative tactics.

Mother's approach was to tell a couple of times and then to smack him. She claimed that she was much more consistent that Mr Fox and that if she made a threat she invariably carried it out. She also admitted however that she was somewhat open to David's manipulative tactics, although not as much as her husband. Generally she felt her husband was much too lenient. Mr Fox admitted this and said that he tended to give in for peace and quiet. He also said that he felt his wife was much too strict.

This had led to a great deal of argument between the parents, primarily because on a number of occasions Mr Fox had countermanded his wife's instructions. Furthermore, he felt that his wife tended to "go on" far too much. Although Mrs Fox admitted this was true, she claimed she was simply trying to get through to David. Both parents admitted that he was well able to play one off against the other and, in addition, that they both in their separate ways sided with David.

Discussion

Both Mr & Mrs Fox were very concerned and caring parents. They readily accepted that David was obtaining a great deal of attention, for instance, through fidgeting, not eating, dawdling in the morning, being untidy, being faddy about his food etc. Both said that they found it very difficult to ignore these and Mrs Fox in particular had a very expressive face which she readily accepted showed her every emotion. Both parents realised the necessity not only to think about ignoring these activities but to practice ignoring over a long period of time.

Parents felt it would be difficult to be firm with him and admitted that because of his difficulties in early childhood (his illness and time in care and their own separations) they had not found it easy to be strict with him. Father in particular admitted that he was trying to make up for difficulties in the past. Mr & Mrs Fox, however, agreed that they needed to act as a team so that David would have the security of firm rules around him. They were motivated anyway, to try to reduce their own arguments.

Luckily, David had shown at home that he was quite responsive to praise. Parents felt that there was a fair chance that he would help in the house so that they could find opportunities to give him attention for acceptable, helpful behaviour. He loved their attention at these times.

Although Mr and Mrs Fox were extremely annoyed by David's fidgeting, his dawdling, his food fads and television addiction they agreed to try to cut down on the attention they gave to these aspects of his behaviour. They resolved to ignore as much as they could and not show emotions on their faces or in their "body language", through being tense.

Follow-up interview

One month later both parents were much more relaxed. They had cut down on David's pocket money. They had fallen into the habit in the past of trying to "buy him off." Although David still attempted to get more money during the week he now accepted their refusal quite calmly. His behaviour had improved in the home and he was no longer having tantrums, was not as noisy or defiant and was tending to cry less. David was still, however, tending to be argumentative on occasions and also stubborn. His mother had been very concerned about him coming in covered in mud and had threatened to make him wash his own clothes. Mrs Fox had not carried this threat out, however, and agreed that being consistent about carrying out threats was an area she would tackle.

The parents generally felt David was much happier and they said there was a definite reduction in marital disagreements. They were trying to work as a team, however, Mrs Fox's father was very ill at that time and this was putting extra strain on the family. They had been trying to find opportunities to praise David and agreed to continue with this over the next few weeks. Ignoring his irritating behaviours had been difficult but Mrs Fox said she was trying to look less upset. David's improved attitude at home was, in any case, helping with this.

Three months later the parents came back for a final interview. Mr Fox said that he and his wife were extremely pleased with David's progress in school. His report had been very good and this was confirmed by the school describing his much more settled behaviour and improved attitude to work. He was no longer staring around the room and calling out and needed very little watching or correction in class. His teacher said that not only had he settled socially but his general conversation had improved. He was saying some quite perceptive things and showing a good general knowledge. He also sang well in the choir.

Mr & Mrs Fox reported that David was showing a great deal more confidence generally. He had passed his cycling proficiency test and had taught himself to swim and to dive. His behaviour in the home continued to improve and also relationships with children his own age. He seemed a much happier and far more contented little boy. The only remaining problem was that his written work remained extremely untidy. David was able to write legibly but tended to take little care after the first couple of lines.

Mr Fox admitted that he had been in the habit of criticising David for this. He fully accepted advice on a more productive way of encouraging David to improve, by praising him for the legible parts.

In view of progress it was agreed that no further appointments would be made. Four years later his difficulties had not re-surfaced at long term follow-up.

Older Children

---

(8) **Colin Hurd**: *He was beginning to show signs of school refusal in his first year in high school, age 12. Note his improved confidence all round as his need for attention was tackled. Note also how his attendance difficulties were tackled as part and parcel of a range of problems stemming from the way he obtained attention at home.*

Colin was referred in the first year of his high school (year 7). He was seen as a quiet well mannered boy who worked to a high standard. Not long after starting school there was a minor incident with a member of staff who shouted at him in front of the class. This so disturbed Colin that he began to be sick every morning before leaving home. Colin seemed very distressed and became terrified of the teacher concerned. He then began to worry about other lessons (Mrs Hurd later said he was also being bullied by prefects in school).

His GP found nothing medically wrong with him and after reassuring Colin his worries seemed to settle. Unfortunately after returning to school after the Christmas holidays his sickness and anxiety started again and he was beginning to over react to any minor reprimands. The school were very worried about him and felt he was "becoming almost paranoid." The GP said that eventually referral to a child psychiatrist might be necessary but after further discussion with school Mr & Mrs Hurd agreed to contact our service.

Colin

Throughout the interview he did not smile very much. He seemed very serious, close to tears, pale and undersized. He made fairly poor eye contact and it was often slightly difficult to understand his speech because of his nervousness.

He said that basically he liked his school and most of his subjects but did not like one teacher who had threatened to "thump him" because he had made a mistake, according to Colin. He said that he had lots of friends at school and no-one was bullying him. His biggest worry was forgetting things when he went to school although he agreed generally he had a reasonable memory. In the mornings before he went out he did not cry and did not have headaches, but felt sick and had an upset feeling in his tummy. Once he got to school these would go away.

At home Colin said that he got on reasonably well with his brother Sam most of the time and enjoyed playing with his bike, playing football or running. He had no particular job to do in the house although he would help from time to time. He could not recall any positive comments from his parents about helping an elderly neighbour on the weekend but he readily remembered being told off for arguing with his brother, being cheeky, not eating, not getting up, leaving things lying about, not coming in on time etc. He said that he could "wangle round" his dad who would tend to give into him but not his mum. When she said no, she meant no. When we discussed ideal parents, he said that in the long run he would prefer them to be strict as if they were soft "I would just play all the time, not do my homework and get into trouble and have accidents."

Parent Interview

Mrs Hurd attended. Colin had normal birth and development and the usual run of childhood ailments. She felt, however, that Colin had not thrived since he had his tonsils and adenoids removed at age seven. For a few days after the operation he had "cried and cried" to go home. When he had eventually returned home he had proved reluctant to speak and refused to eat. Investigations showed that his throat had turned septic but even when this cleared up his mum felt that he was not really thriving.

Pre-school, Colin was a good mixer but with a tendency to wander away. He settled well to nursery and infant school and then for most of juniors. In the year 5, however, although a good footballer, one particular boy began putting pressure on him not to play so well so that he himself could shine. Colin began to show anxiety but when mother investigated and encouraged him to do his best, matters settled.

When he went to his high school, his brother who had intended to stay on at school left. This upset Colin who had

been looking forward to his brother's support. He began being sick in school during his second week. The GP prescribed medication for "nerves" but then Colin began to show extreme reluctance to even leave the house to play. Mum had managed to maintain regular attendance at school for Colin but with difficulty.

Personality

According to Mrs Hurd, Colin was a rather unhappy child. He could, however, show a good sense of humour and was truthful. At times he was cheeky and rather moody, he was also noisy and active (mother tended to go on about this). He was not too stubborn but did tend to be defiant and argumentative, more so with mother than father. He was an affectionate child but reluctant to discuss problems in fact "everything has to be dragged out of him." Colin would help in the house but was rarely asked. His mother felt that he looked for a great deal of attention and that he also seemed immature and also inclined to cry very easily if checked. He had little patience and panicked if faced with difficult tasks. Basically she felt he lacked confidence. His relationship with his brother, Sam, was quite reasonable with some arguments. Sam had for some years maintained that Colin was thoroughly spoiled.

Colin was a nail biter and also inclined to "stretch his mouth." His father, in particular, paid a great deal of attention to both these habits. His appetite was good but he constantly complained about his dinners and disliked vegetables. Mrs Hurd, in the past, had tried persuasion, but now claimed that she had given this up as a bad job. He was rather reluctant to go to bed on time and this led to a great deal of fuss in the house. He always dawdled in the mornings and this also brought a great deal of attention from his mum.

Management

Mrs Hurd said that she rather lacked patience and that her approach with Colin was to tell the boy two or three times before making threats which she always carried out. Her husband seemed to be more patient but his approach was to reason and then tell Colin, then make threats, but then not usually carry these out. In Mrs Hurd's opinion her husband was much too lenient with both children when they were younger.

Discussion

Mrs Hurd admitted she was a born worrier and admitted she had tended to fuss round Colin a lot. She had quite naturally been concerned about him after his hospitalisation and she agreed with his brother that, as he was the youngest, both parents had tended to spoil him and not make any demands on him at home.

She fairly readily agreed that Colin was creaming off attention because of his irritating habits. As she had not provided many opportunities for him to earn approval in the house, they had become rather locked into a vicious cycle of just emphasising the matters the family were worried about - such as sickness and his irritating habits. Mrs Hurd agreed that it would be useful to "tighten up" with Colin and in fact said her husband recently appeared to have been making an effort in that area. Although he could not attend, she agreed to pass on our

discussion to him and try to agree on both of them acting more as a team.

Mum readily agreed to try to get her and her husband to follow a similar standard of low key but effective discipline and to ignore the minor irritating behaviours Colin produced. Most importantly, we discussed the need to try to find him little jobs to do around the house, in order to create opportunities to praise him and provide positive attention.

Follow-up

Mrs Hurd said that things were a lot better. Colin still seemed rather anxious on the days he had the teacher who he was most afraid of, but other mornings he was getting up for school without any trouble. He seemed to be mixing more freely with other children and seemed happier in himself.

After examining the past few weeks in detail, it turned out that parents had not, however, gone out of their way to find many jobs for him to do. We discussed again the need to attempt this to build up Colin's confidence through praise and encouragement and how tasks in the home gave a good opportunity to provide these.

Mrs Hurd said that she herself lacked confidence and said that she did not want Colin to suffer as she had. She was therefore fairly motivated to carry on with what she had begun and had been pleased to see signs of progress already.

At a further interview, Mrs Hurd confirmed that the programme was now running well. She and her husband had made a special effort to praise Colin and to set their rules down together and stick to them. She reported that Colin's behaviour and attitudes to school had continued to improve and after the Easter break he had re-started school without any difficulty. His head of year reported that Colin seemed much happier and had not been reporting sick. He was arranging for Colin to get back on the football team.

Three years later the case had not been re-referred. At long term follow-up, his parents reported that Colin had taken up a paper round and that he was saving and controlling his own pocket money. He was happy and settled in school.

(9) **Philip Gardner**: *He was making poor progress in school and displaying behaviour difficulties at home age 12. Note that despite previous help the basic problem had not been tackled. Note also how the difficulties in dealing with his behaviour spilled over into his reading sessions. See also how he "switched tactics" when his parents began to tackle the problems though he gradually settled and his work improved at school.*

Philip had originally been referred to the department of child and family psychiatry about two years previously by his family GP. He had been displaying both learning and behaviour difficulties. He attended the unit for about a year and his reading progressed to a certain extent, he worked hard and, according to his parents, he loved going. He was discharged from the unit but his behaviour began to deteriorate. He was referred by school to the psychology service because of concern about his behaviour at home and poor progress. He was a boy of average intelligence but when seen at age twelve years had a reading age of about eight.

Philip

In discussion, Philip was quite an attractive lad with a friendly approach. He admitted to finding reading difficult but said that he generally liked school. He also said that reading sessions at home were rather upsetting. Mrs Gardner confirmed this in our discussion with her where she said that Mr Gardner would try to help Philip with his reading. He would tend to lose his temper, criticise him for mistakes and go on for a long time (an understandable difficulty where parents are very concerned about reading).

Parent Interview

Mrs Gardner attended. Philip had a younger brother Harry. Philip had settled in quite well to his high school but in the last two weeks he had been claiming illness in an attempt to avoid attending.

Personality

According to Mrs Gardner, Philip was a happy, truthful, honest boy with a good sense of humour. He could, however, be rather moody for no apparent reason and he was also extremely noisy and active in the home (this tended to get both parents down). Philip, like his brother, was always "on the want" and liked his own way. He could be stubborn, contrary and very argumentative. He did not "harp on" and would quite willingly wait to have his wants satisfied, but he rather resented discipline and had on occasions told his mother that he hated her. If he was refused his own way or thwarted in any way he would indulge in tantrums. In Mrs Gardner's opinion, Philip was a sensitive boy who tried hard to hide his feelings. If father shouted at him he would be reduced to tears.

Philip would help in the house voluntarily and showed a good response to praise, according to his mother. If he was interested in a task he showed a fair amount of patience but he did have a low tolerance of frustration and seemed to lack confidence. Generally, about the house, he was quite tidy.

Relationships with his brother, Harry, were not very good partly because Harry was rather bossy. Mrs Gardner suspected that Philip could be fairly afraid of Harry but now, however, he was starting to turn on him. With other children outside Philip was unable to stick up for himself. Unfortunately, he had an explosive temper if pushed too far.

In the home Philip was very fidgety. Mother claimed that she could ignore this but admitted that it irritated her. His appetite was "fantastic."

Management

When it came to discipline in the home there was a regular contact with the grandmother who was very indulgent with a tendency to interfere with the parents discipline. Mrs Gardner said that she had a fair amount of patience and that her approach was "to give a couple of warnings" before resorting to threats which she did not always carry out. She admitted that she was rather vulnerable to Philip's manipulative tactics. She said that her husband had little patience and he would also give a couple of warnings but then resorted to threats which were not always carried out either. The two had not always backed each other up over disciplinary matters with the result that Philip had played one off against the other. She admitted that on occasions she had covered up for him "to stop him from getting wrong" and this had caused a great deal of arguments between the parents and had led Mr Gardner to accuse his wife of being too lenient.

Philip was fairly settled in their new house, but had regularly complained at their old house that children were picking on him and he would come in crying. He tended to wander and just "turn up" and not understand the upset that this caused his parents. Mrs Gardner saw him as easily led. At his previous school, his grandparents had been caretakers and it was felt that part of the difficulty was that in the evenings he had the run of the school and felt he should have that during the day also.

Currently, his class teacher was worried about him being "naughty" in class, not sitting down getting on with his work and then interfering with the other children's' activities. He had been soiling at home when in juniors although this had diminished in the high school. His junior school teacher apparently had mentioned hyperactivity to his parents because of his restlessness. The GP had not accepted this although the parents had been give a diet sheet.

The interview with Mrs Gardner focused partly on Philip's behaviour at home and also partly on the parents approach to helping him with reading.

She showed insight into the way Philip had been obtaining a great deal of attention at home and agreed to tackle this.

Mrs Gardner readily saw the logic in ignoring the minor, silly misbehaviours which irritated her and her husband such as fidgeting. She also appreciated the need for her and her husband to come to a better understanding over discipline, and to avoid arguments between themselves. She said she would try to cut down on the idle threats, not cover up for Philip and discuss with Mr Gardner a clearer approach, with small, quick, early punishments that they would carry through. As Philip would happily help around the house, mum was quite willing to use such occasions as opportunities to praise him.

Following some examination of the stresses involved in Philip's current reading sessions, mum also agreed to try to take a more low key approach to reading and to use lots of cuddles (see Ann Miller's case study for more details of this "Cuddle and Read" approach).

Follow-up

About one month later, Mrs Gardner reported that she was beginning to ignore much of Philip's aggravating and irritating behaviour. She said "I found it easier to ignore him that I thought it would be." Mr Gardner was also co-operating with this.

Dad had taken up fishing and had arranged to take Philip with him on Fridays. Philip enjoyed this and his parents were using this as an encouragement for his behaviour during the week.

There were still signs that Philip was getting attention for misbehaviour, however, and had switched his tactics. He now tended to dawdle over his breakfast and would not leave for school until the last possible minute. Previously, he had gained attention by leaving too early. Furthermore, he had taken to losing his temper more with his brother.

Philip was still tending to wander and had taken to going to the next town with friends and not telling his parents. Mrs Gardner felt that she had perhaps been over-protective with him and by discouraging him from going out had in fact created a problem. She now felt she ought to give Philip more freedom as he had demonstrated that he could take responsibility in the sense of looking after himself and catching the correct buses.

On the whole there were pleasing signs of improvement with Philip, and his reading had started to make progress and he was showing growing interest. We reinforced the need to carry on with the approaches to both his reading and his behaviour, particularly to concentrate on ignoring the new irritating behaviours which had appeared.

A further appointment was arranged a month later and mother reported that she was pleased to find that he had been making much greater progress that she had hoped for. His class teacher had been very complimentary about his reading and his behaviour had settled.

At home he was also much happier although he still had his odd off days. His father had been in the habit of responding to Philip's annoying habits previously, but now was following advice and beginning to ignore a great deal of Philip's irritating aspects. Mrs Gardner said that she was no longer so protective of Philip and she allowed him to go to the swimming pool and to take his brother and supervise him (he was a non-swimmer). So far Philip had not let her down.

Matters gradually settled and 2 years later the case had not been re-referred and Philip's behaviour was still acceptable at home at long term follow-up.

(10) **John Utting**: *He was showing early signs of delinquency at age 13. Note how his glue sniffing was tackled as part of a larger range of difficulties and how his behaviour and school work all improved together.*

Background

John was referred by his mother. He was a year 8 pupil at high school, age 13. His parents said they were "finding him difficult to understand." He had been shoplifting but had not yet been prosecuted. He admitted to his mother that he had been glue sniffing.

John

John was a blonde attractive rogue with a nice smile. He said that he enjoyed the school and that he had a lot of friends there and no particular dislikes. He liked football, riding motor bikes and BMX bikes and when he left school he wanted to be a footballer or professional snooker player. John admitted that he had been picked up by the police for stealing a pen from a newsagents in town with some friends, but claimed it was the first time.

At home John said that he would do a number of jobs for his parents such as cleaning up. The last job he could remember was cleaning three pairs of shoes the previous day. He could not recall any praise for this. He was very honest about his misbehaviour at home and said that he was "not an angel." He readily volunteered that he was often in trouble for being untidy and noisy, arguing, being cheeky, coming in late and fidgeting. It was clear that John was receiving a fair amount of attention at home for various unacceptable behaviours.

When we discussed discipline John said that he could soft soap his mum but not his dad. We discussed whether it was better for him as he was growing up to have strict or lenient parents. He said that "if you have soft ones you'll get into a lot of trouble, go to court, etc., if they don't check on what you're doing, homework and so on." In other words in the long run he quite readily accepted that parents should be strict (this in fact is quite common in children of his age). Furthermore, when asked whether he would prefer a short sharp punishment and have the matter over and done with and no more said or to be nagged at for hours on end (and possibly even avoid the punishment) he quite quickly chose the quick punishment.

Parent Interview

Mrs Utting said he had a normal birth and childhood with only the usual run of childhood ailments.

Pre-school John was a good mixer and he settled well at nursery. In his last term, however, he took a marked dislike to the nursery and when he began attending primary school he screamed when left by his mother. He settled, however, after a couple of weeks. At eleven, he entered the high school and again settled reasonably well. His brother was at that time attending the school also and according to Mrs Utting "he kept John out of scrapes." John was attending school when we saw mum, but with a marked lack of enthusiasm.

Personality

According to Mrs Utting John was a happy, truthful boy with a good sense of humour. He did, however, have moods for no apparent reason. He had in the past taken money from home but this appeared to be confined mainly to odd coins lying about. John later readily admitted this and it would appear the family did not really regard this as "stealing."

While John was not unduly demanding he did like all his own way and if denied it was inclined to indulge in minor tantrums. He was often stubborn and contrary but not usually defiant or very argumentative. He appeared "resigned to discipline", nevertheless, he often claimed that he was being picked on.

He was an affectionate boy to both parents but did not find it easy to discuss his worries. John was also quite a sensitive lad and easily reduced to tears. He was relatively quiet in the house and could occupy himself and had a reasonable amount of patience when interested. His mother felt, however, he generally lacked confidence when out and about. His relationship with his brother was good and with other children he managed to stick up for himself.

John was fairly fussy about meals and his mother invariably tried to persuade him and in the end had to cater specifically for him.

Management

Mrs Utting said that she was fairly patient and that her approach was "to tell three times and then 'crack' him." She claimed that she always carried out her threats. However, after further discussion, mum did admit that she was rather vulnerable to John's manipulative tactics. Father had much more patience that Mrs Utting but he also had a tendency to make threats and not carry them out and in addition he was also vulnerable to John's manipulative tactics. Mrs Utting felt that her husband "could be too soft." Furthermore, she felt that he "should support me in my decision." Mr Utting had occasionally countermanded her in front of the boy which had resulted in arguments between the parents. He had also criticised her "about going on at both of the children all the time about the state of the house." It came out in further discussion that in fact mum rarely asked John to help in the house.

Discussion

Mrs Utting was quite receptive to suggestions that she and her husband needed to adopt a clearer and agreed approach to discipline with John which involved early punishment with few threats and little attention being fed in. She was helped to get over her feeling of guilt over punishing him by hearing John's own comments about his attitudes to strict and lenient parents.

As mentioned above Mrs Utting quickly saw the need to find opportunities to praise and encourage John as a way of boosting his confidence and also to feed in attention for appropriate activities in the house and to relieve some of the tension of having to complain about untidiness. More minor irritating matters she would ignore.

Follow-up

About one month later Mrs Utting said "there has been a great improvement" in John's behaviour. After the initial interview she had discussed our ideas with her husband who at first had not agreed. In view of the improvement, however, he was now wholeheartedly co-operating.

Mrs Utting said that she had had difficulty in carrying out the ideas initially but had keep it up and was now extremely pleased with the results. John was now much more helpful in the house and on a couple of occasions, for instance, had done a great deal of ironing. Parents had found many opportunities such as this to praise him. They had also begun to agree their rules and carry out their punishments without arguments. John had accepted this. Mum said she no longer needed to hit him. Mr and Mrs Utting had found ignoring John's minor, irritating behaviours relatively easy.

In Mrs Utting's opinion John was now a far happier child. She felt the improvement had generalised so that the whole family appeared to be more contented.

John's attitude to school work had also changed for the better. Over the last few weeks he had consistently earned at least one merit mark each week which delighted his mother. In addition he seemed to be increasing in confidence although there seemed to be some evidence of getting bullied at school. We agreed that she should discuss this with his head of year.

Six months later school confirmed that his behaviour there was quite acceptable and he was showing an improved attitude generally. Two and a half years later, John was still settled at home and school at long term follow-up.

(11) **Peter Hart**: *Age 14, school were very worried about his tendency to use physical aggression. Note how Peter could recall very little in the way of praise to begin with. Note also how the whole family relationship improved and Peter's attitude at school changed as his attention seeking was tackled.*

Peter was referred by his high school at age fourteen for aggressive behaviour towards children and staff. He had been charged with assault and was due to go to court.

Peter

He was quite clearly coping relatively well with school work within his ability level. Although initially giving a hostile impression he warmed up during the interview and showed a pleasant, friendly side to his nature. He was positive about his school and said basically his ideal teacher would be strict, but fair. He had been involved in several fights and did not particularly like getting involved but "could not walk away."

At home Peter carried out a number of jobs such as running messages, cleaning out the rabbit hutch, tidying up, making the tea and so on. He had made the tea and tidied up the previous night and could only recall from his parents a simple "thank you." He could well recall a great deal of argument and criticism whenever he misbehaved, however.

When we discussed his parents approach to discipline at home Peter quite clearly said he would prefer short, sharp punishment to being nagged at. He admitted that he would often try to "wangle round" his mum and he would often be successful. When she became really annoyed however she "showed that she meant it" and Peter said, "when she starts, she's a bad'un." He did not dare to try to wangle round his dad and his mum often tried to protect him from his father.

Parent Interview

Both parents attended. Peter had a normal early childhood and settled well to primary school. He was initially enthusiastic about his split site comprehensive high school, but his behaviour deteriorated when he moved to the main school site after a couple of years.

Personality

According to Mr and Mrs Hart, Peter was quite a happy, honest, truthful boy with a good sense of humour. He could be quite stubborn and argumentative (but not with father). He would help in the house if asked but seemed embarrassed if praised. Mrs Hart felt he was a rather sensitive boy who tried to hide his feelings but he could show affection.

Peter was untidy and had little patience and a low tolerance of frustration. He also lacked confidence. If told off or denied, he would sulk. Mrs Hart said she often gave in to his demands to avoid sulking.

He had a good appetite but was fairly fussy about his food and his mother would cook especially for him. He had a number of interests but would soon become bored with one and then would want to change to another.

Peter had particularly irritating habits which triggered off his mother, of nail biting, picking his nose and dawdling in the morning.

Management

Mr Hart presented as a tough "no-nonsense" man. He said that he had little patience and that his approach was to tell Peter once, whereupon the boy obeyed.

Mrs Hart said she was a born worrier and that her approach to discipline was to go on and on at him before making threats which were not always carried out. She felt that her husband was much too strict and that in the past he had smacked the boy quite unnecessarily. At times she had protected Peter by jumping in front of him to keep his father from him. She had also criticised Mr Hart in front of the boy. She had on occasions worked with Peter to undermine his father's requests. For instance, when Mr Hart had told Peter to stay in, she had let him go out, then told him to return home before his father came back. These disagreements over handling had led to arguments between Mr and Mrs Hart.

Mr Hart felt his wife was too lenient with Peter and too over-protective. She, however, said that she had been forced into this by her husband's strictness. He claimed that he was not strict and that he had only ever hit the boy on the shoulders or arms.

Discussion

During the course of the interview, Mr and Mrs Hart gradually relaxed. They showed clearly that they were caring parents. They quite openly discussed their attitudes to each other's approach to discipline and agreed that they would try to seek a more happy compromise. Mrs Hart would try to trust her husband to keep his promise not to hit Peter. Mrs Hart also agreed to try to be less protective towards him - he was an only child and she had always worried about him since being a baby because of a small medical problem he had had with his spine. She was somewhat relieved to hear our report of Peter's comments about how he felt discipline should be handled. Parents agreed to try smaller, non-physical punishments such as grounding him or stopping his TV.

Both parents accepted that Peter could be very irritating to them through his habits, such as nail biting. Mother in particular found these a constant source of annoyance. They accepted that it would be difficult to ignore these, but the effort was worth it to reduce the attention he gained. Mr and Mrs Hart felt it would also be difficult to show Peter lots of praise (neither parents had been very confident at showing emotion) but agreed to try to do this to give him regular positive attention in the house.

Follow-up Interview

One month later Mr and Mrs Hart reported that "things have been great at home and outside."

Mrs Hart said that she had made an effort and had changed her way of dealing with Peter. Mr Hart disagreed. After some discussion he began to see more clearly his wife's position. He then began to talk more about expressing his own feelings towards his wife and Peter.

Peter's behaviour was looked at in more detail. He was by then seen as much more helpful in the home and less stubborn and argumentative. Mrs Hart said she was much more happier with him and had found she could be less protective towards him. Mr Hart found that he and Peter now seemed to have a much closer relationship - whereas previously the lad would avoid him he had now taken to sitting and chatting with him. Mr Hart was obviously very pleased about this, he said: "You know, he'll come and sit next to me now."

Parents had been able to praise him much more and Peter had, in fact, greatly appreciated this despite initially seeming embarrassed. Mr Hart had not hit Peter and mum had backed him up over punishments such as keeping Peter in. The nail biting, nose picking and dawdling had all begun to diminish when parents had ignored these.

A further follow-up one month later revealed that Peter was very readily working at home now on his homework, without even having to be asked. He had settled well at school and had apparently come top in maths which was taken by the teacher who he had previously had his worst relationships with. Peter had been living up to his mum's trust at home. When he had been going out he had not been drinking cider with the local children or mixing with glue sniffers.

Peter left school two years later, without further referral, with six GCSE passes. He managed to find a job and two years after that was still quite settled when we called in to chat to the family at long term follow-up.

(12) **Sandra Telfer**: *Age 16, she was attending a school for children with severe learning difficulties. She started refusing to go to school. Note how the main problem of school attendance was not tackled on its own, but by tackling the whole range of difficulties she displayed.*

Sandra was a sixteen year old girl with Down's syndrome. She was relatively able in school but had little conversation. She had a heart murmur. She had two sisters, ten years older. Her father was an accountant and her mother was at home. Attendance problems led us to having a discussion in school.

Parents Interview

Sandra could be happy and loving at home but also moody and would often whinge. She used to be quite keen on jigsaws and looking at books, and used to play a lot on her own, but had recently become inactive. Mr and Mrs Telfer for a long time had not felt they could "push her" because of her heart condition, but they were now finding

that she would not even walk a couple of steps from the car. While on holiday she also used pains in her tummy to manipulate them back into the car to listen to the radio. Sandra also irritated them when they took her to Blackpool by refusing to watch the lights when they finally got there.

Sandra's periods started a couple of years ago and although Mr and Mrs Telfer at first thought that might have triggered off her difficulties, there were signs of problems well before that. She now liked her own way and could be obstinate and defiant. In the mornings she refused to get dressed. She had a number of irritating habits, for instance she would ask her parents for a drink and yet have to be told several times to drink it. She also had to be coaxed to eat. It was a great struggle to get her to bed and they had to leave her until she was tired out.

Both parents said that they tried to be patient with her, but admitted that they easily became exasperated. If they tried to persuade her to do something she did not want to do, she would dig her heels in. During the discussion, Mr and Mrs Telfer admitted that they had been somewhat lax and over-indulgent in the past and although she enjoyed praise, they readily admitted that they had not made a point of emphasising this.

After looking at the possible ways Sandra could be getting attention for inappropriate behaviour, her parents agreed to try to be firmer with her generally and to ignore any minor problems. At the same time they resolved to give her attention when they decided to, when she was behaving in a positive manner at home.

The refusing to go to school was seen as just one amongst a collection of attention seeking ploys. By tackling all of these problems at once, Mr and Mrs Telfer would create a positive climate where their attempts at getting her to school would be more likely to succeed.

Follow-up Interview

A few weeks later, Mr Telfer said "there had been a transformation." Both parents said that they had been making an effort to praise her and had been ignoring a lot of the silly irritating things such as not drinking when they had brought her a cup of tea. Her parents had also "tightened up" their discipline, although not in a heavy handed way and had found that Sandra was much more active and interested in playing at home. She was also happier and generally smiling more. She appeared less stubborn, and for instance was going to bed more readily. There was also a great deal less crying and whinging.

Sandra was not refusing to dress and was not complaining the minute she got out of the car and had to walk. There were no more tantrums, although she could still be a little irritating at meal times by not eating very readily.

Mrs Cairns, her class teacher, said that Sandra's attendance had improved greatly and she appeared to be showing a much better attitude to school. She was coming willingly and settling in rapidly. She appeared to be enjoying the lessons more and interacting better with other children. There were still occasional tears during the day but she seemed to get over these much more quickly. Mrs Cairns had used a home-school diary to emphasise positive comments about Sandra to parents. Sandra had obviously enjoyed the fact that home and school were communicating about her in a very positive manner.

Sandra had not been referred again three years later. She left school and was still settled at our final long term follow-up visit.

Further reading and references

There are very few books which concentrate on attention seeking at home. M. Balson's "Becoming a better parent" (published by Hodder and Stoughton, 1987) provides some suggestions.

Attention seeking in school, practical approaches to it and some of the theory behind the problem, is covered in detail in my previous book "Attention seeking: a practical solution for the classroom" (published by Lucky Duck, 1997).

Excellent texts for parents which look at behaviour management generally, include C. Green's "Toddler Taming" (published by Century, 1987), "Label with care" by T. Bliss (published by Lucky Duck, 1998) and "Help! I've got a kid!" by W. Bartz and R. Rasor (published by Exley, 1987).

"Behaviour can Change" by E.V.S. Westmacott and R.J. Cameron for more on "Fuzzies." (published by MacMillan 1981).

ADHD can be explored in "Understanding attention deficit disorder" by C. Green and K. Chee (published by Vermillion, 1995) or "The ADHD handbook" by A. Munden and J. Arcelus (published by Jessica Kingsley, 1999).

Two books which are very critical of the use of Ritalin for ADHD are "Toxic psychiatry" by P. Breggin (published by Harper Collins, 1991) and "Ritalin Nation" by R. DeGrandpre (published by W.W.Norton, 1999).

For problem solving and conflict resolution ideas see "Parent Effectiveness" (published by Plume Books, 1975) and "Teaching Children Self Discipline" (published by Times Books, New York, 1989) both by Thomas Gordon.

Other books mentioned in the text, which are aimed mainly at professionals, are:

R. Morgan "Behavioural Treatments with Children" (published by William Heinemann Medical Books Ltd., 1984).

G.W. LaVigna and A.M. Donnellan "Alternatives to Punishment" (published by Irvington publishers, 1986).

C. Webster-Stratton and M. Herbert "Troubled Families - Problem Children" (published by Chichester, 1994).

Some of these books may be out of print by now, but library copies may be available.

Attention Seeking

A practical solution for the Classroom

By Nigel Mellor

"Off Task - Out of Seat - Talking Out of Turn - Troubling Other Children!"
It is the high frequency of these behaviours by a few pupils which makes it hard for teachers to manage the behaviour of the whole class.
This publication is the first to address these specific behaviours and to provide teachers with a clear and simple set of strategies to:

- Assess the problem
- Relate targets to IEPs
- Reduce the unwanted behaviours
- Increase the desired behaviours

The book was reprinted within weeks due to demand. All teachers face this problem in every classroom.

ISBN 1 873942 76 1
Price £12.00

Reviews of Attention Seeking:

"I Immediately felt a lot of empathy. All-in-all an excellent book." Special

*"Help is now at hand… for the teachers… driven to despair"*Times Educational Supplement

*"Practical strategies [to counter these] weapons of mass disruption"*The Guardian

*"… even makes enjoyable bedtime reading, since Mellor's style is easy and interesting… case studies… bring this book alive"*Special Children

*"… good, sound advice… for those involved in teacher training"*Educational Psychology in Practice

*"An abundance of common sense"*Education and Health

"… for the harassed teacher… invaluable" Child Care Forum

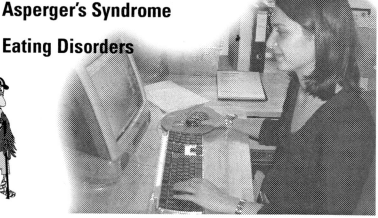